The Death Penalty

Sanjeev P. Sahni · Mohita Junnarkar

The Death Penalty

Perspectives from India and Beyond

Springer

Sanjeev P. Sahni
Jindal Institute of Behavioural Sciences
O. P. Jindal Global University
Sonipat, Haryana, India

Mohita Junnarkar
Jindal Institute of Behavioural Sciences
O. P. Jindal Global University
Sonipat, Haryana, India

ISBN 978-981-15-3128-6 ISBN 978-981-15-3129-3 (eBook)
https://doi.org/10.1007/978-981-15-3129-3

This Springer imprint is published by the registered company Springer Nature Singapore Pte Ltd.
The registered company address is: 152 Beach Road, #21-01/04 Gateway East, Singapore 189721, Singapore

The authors are indebted to Mr. Mohak Kapoor and Ms. Aviva Jogani for their extraordinary efforts for methodically compiling the research study. Without their contribution and support, this book would not have been completed.

Foreword

The use of violence, even lethal violence, to establish, protect, defend, and impose one's rights, dominion, and power over others has been part of human history since its beginning. According to the seventeenth-century English philosopher Thomas Hobbes, widely regarded as one of a few truly great political philosophers as his masterwork Leviathan rivals in significance the political writings of Plato, Aristotle, Locke, Rousseau, Kant, and Rawls, the "state of nature" for humans is one of widespread violence to defend oneself from the dominion and depredations of others, affirm one's possessions and interests, and ensure one's self-preservation. Life for humans entails the "natural right to do anything one thinks necessary for preserving one's own life." Thus, the human condition per se is one of constant war, and life is "solitary, poor, nasty, brutish, and short" (Leviathan, Chapters XIII–XIV). According to Hobbes, humans finally entered into a "social contract" limiting one's rights to power, possessions, and unlimited freedom to act as each wished, in exchange for the tranquil enjoyment of what one has and has been able to build and for assurances that it cannot be taken from him or her by someone else simply because he is more powerful and better able to defeat others. To escape from this constantly uncertain, violent, and menacing situation, humans accepted limits on themselves and agreed to give their government even absolute power. Punishment, including the death penalty, became then the needed and justified mechanism for the government to protect and enforce the social contract governing human relations. The first written death penalty laws date as far back as the eighteenth century B.C. in the Code of King Hammurabi of Babylon, which codified the death penalty for 25 different crimes.

There is no question that the death penalty was widely used throughout human history in all parts of the world and often delivered in cruel and debasing ways, stripping the condemned of their human dignity and subjecting them to torture and ample pain.

The use of the death penalty for an ever increasing list of crimes was justified as not being a violation of the offender's right to life because he or she had forfeited that right by perpetrating the crime and breaking the "social contract." Thus, the death penalty was and is considered justifiable as a morally permissible way to respond forcefully to criminal behavior and discourage others from engaging in it, thus protecting society's interests.

An important principle governing how to respond to criminal victimization is the "lex talionis" that specifies defined penalties for specific crimes, mostly based on full reciprocity. In the Hammurabi legal code, the principle of exact reciprocity is very clearly stated and operationalized. For example, if a person caused the death of another person, the killer would be put to death.

Often a religious justification has been invoked to justify the adoption and imposition of the death penalty and to formulate penalties for specific crimes. Some propose that this was at least in part intended to prevent excessive punishment at the hands of either an avenging private party or the state. The most common expression of lex talionis is "an eye for an eye," but other interpretations have been given as well. Legal codes following the principle of lex talionis have one thing in common: they prescribe "fitting" counter punishment for a felony. In the legal code written by Hammurabi, the principle of exact reciprocity is very clearly used. The simplest example is the "eye for an eye" principle. In that case, the rule is that punishment must be exactly equal to the crime. This is clearly expressed in the book of Leviticus in the Hebrew Bible: "And a man who injures his countryman – as he has done, so it shall be done to him [namely,] fracture for fracture, eye for eye, tooth for tooth. Just as another person has received injury from him, so it will be given to him" (Lev. 24:19–21). The principle is also mentioned in Deuteronomy and Exodus. This norm has been interpreted by some as actually softening and limiting the excesses that feuds and vendettas did generate when retribution was carried out. Even further, the Talmud interprets the verses referring to "an eye for an eye" and similar expressions as requiring monetary compensation in tort cases, contradicting a different interpretation by the Sadducees that the Bible verses refer only to physical retaliation in kind. Throughout history, the lex talionis or "Law of Retaliation" has also been presented as actually a quite benign and positive development, requiring that the law establishes and the offender provides equitable retribution.

In Islam, the Qu'ran (5:45) mentions the "eye for an eye" concept as mandatory for the Children of Israel. The principle of Lex talionis in Islam is Qi ā (Qur'an, 2:178). Muslim countries that apply Islamic Sharia law, such as Iran or Saudi Arabia, apply the "eye for an eye" rule literally.

However, in Christianity, in the Sermon on the Mount, Jesus actually urges his followers to turn the other cheek: "You have heard that it was said, 'An eye for an eye and a tooth for a tooth.' But I say to you, Do not resist the one who is evil. But if anyone slaps you on the right cheek, turn to him the other also" (Matthew 5:38–39). However, in reality, since it is also part of Christianity's holy books, the Hebrew Bible's mandate has had a preponderant practical influence.

It was not until the eighteenth century that the Enlightenment in Europe began to underline the value of human beings, started to talk about human rights, and demanded limits against the excessive authority of kings. It eventually inspired the French Revolution that also stressed freedom, equality, and fraternity. It was at that time that challenges to the excessive punishments imposed by the criminal justice system of the time began to appear. One of the most talented jurist and greatest thinkers of the Age of Enlightenment, Cesare Beccaria (1738-1794), wrote his manifesto "On Crimes and Punishments". This slim book, initially published anonymously for fear of repercussions, strongly criticized and rejected arbitrary and cruel punishment which was the most common tool the state used at that time to terrorize people into submission, especially to prevent and discourage any rebellion challenging the hierarchical structure of the society.

The fundamental questions that Beccaria asked were: "What is the function of punishment?" and "If a person perpetrates a crime, how should we punish him or her?" He replied to the first by rejecting revenge and retribution and stressing instead prevention and dissuasion from committing the crime. As to punishment, referring to the social contract, he stated that punishment is justified only to protect and defend the social contract and to motivate everyone to abide by it. He stressed that it should be swift, as opposed to long detention awaiting trial, to build a clear connection between crime and its punishment; certain, so as to have dissuading and preventative value; and most of all proportional to the crime committed to avoid excessive and cruel punishment. He cogently argued that crimes "are more effectually prevented by the certainty than by the severity of the punishment." Moreover, Beccaria was definitely against torture, arguing that it may torment the criminal but not deter future offenders, and against the death penalty. He was one of the first thinkers to write a logical and sustained critique of the use of the death penalty. While the death penalty has been used worldwide in history, Beccaria stated that "the ultimate punishment has never deterred men determined to harm society." As a matter of fact, he pointed out that the state uses its most draconian measures when crime is at its highest levels. He also reasoned that replying to savagery with state-sponsored savagery negates the "general humaneness of civil society." Overall, Beccaria maintained that the state has little legitimacy when imposing the death penalty and that doing so is really not an especially useful policy. Beccaria's approach was very influential at the time, including in the newly formed United States, and it continued being so throughout the centuries since his death. Recent policies he impacted include, but are not limited to, truth in sentencing, swift punishment, and the abolition of the death penalty in some states in the United States. For example, the state of Michigan abolished it as early as 1846 (except for treason).

The death penalty continues to be applied in a number of countries and the debate over its use has increased, especially after the middle of the twentieth century when important legal, social, and humane principles were enshrined in international declarations and conventions under the auspices of international organizations like the United Nations, the Organization of American States, and the Council of Europe. Examples are the Universal Declaration of Human Rights (1948), the American Declaration on the Rights and Duties of Man (1948), the European Convention for the Protection of Human Rights and Fundamental Freedoms (1950), the International Covenant on Civil and Political Rights (1966), and the American Convention on Human Rights (1968). The establishment of the European Court of Human Rights (1959) and of the Inter American Court of Human Rights (1979) greatly strengthened the recognition and application of human rights and among them, the right to life. Thus, the argument is that the death penalty is a violation of the most fundamental human right—the right to life. It represents the ultimate cruel, inhuman, and degrading punishment. Another powerful argument is that the death penalty is imposed in a discriminatory way. For example, in the United States and others, the death penalty was often utilized in rape cases, but especially when the defendant was African-American and the victim white. Poor people without the financial means to defend themselves effectively, and especially members of minority groups, received the death penalty disproportionately when compared to white people. This is also because when in 1976 the Supreme Court reinstated the death penalty in the United States, it allowed the possibility of using it not only for murder but also for rape and armed robbery, thus multiplying the situations when it could be meted out.

Another serious objection to the death penalty is based on its finality. Someone who is innocent can be released from prison if there is evidence to overturn the conviction. However, an execution cannot be reversed.

The often touted deterrent effect of the death penalty has also been seriously and empirically disputed. However, powerful beliefs and stereotypes persist, strengthened by racial prejudice and class status.

Opposing the death penalty is still a risky move. On November 8, 1988, the governor of Massachusetts USA, Michael Dukakis, was defeated in the presidential election by George W. Bush in part because Dukakis opposed the death penalty and supported a prison furlough program meant to be rehabilitative. Unfortunately, an inmate incarcerated for murder did commit a series of crimes, including rape, right after he was furloughed.

Another argument against the death penalty often mentioned is its cost especially in countries like the United States where lengthy appeals are common, costing the taxpayer considerably.

Currently, a major point of debate and opposition to the death penalty is on how it is carried out. Hanging, the electric chair, and the firing squad have been discontinued in many jurisdictions in favor of the use of a cocktail of medicines that induces death. Because of the refusal of the medical profession to participate in executions since it would violate the Hippocratic oath governing the practice of medicine, executions using drugs are carried out by prison employees, resulting at times in botched executions that violate the human right against cruel and unusual punishment. Moreover, many drug suppliers under pressure by opponents of the death penalty are refusing to supply the needed drugs. Thus, many executions have been placed on hold. Recently, the state of Oklahoma in the United States has announced the resumption of executions because it has reportedly secured a reliable source of the chemicals needed.

This volume, The Death Penalty: Perspectives from India and Beyond, authored by Sanjeev P. Sahni and Mohita Junnarkar, represents a substantial and needed contribution to the international debate about the death penalty. First, it places the discourse on the death penalty within a global context. In a useful way, it offers an overview of the current use, debate, and application of the death penalty in Africa, the Americas, the Asia Pacific, the Middle East, and Europe and, finally, in the area of major focus of this book, India. This is a very valuable update on the status of the death penalty and related developments worldwide, a much needed global summary that provides context and analysis and builds the foundation for a clear and well-founded understanding of the main focus of the book: the status and application of the death penalty in India. The authors and their team deserve to be strongly congratulated for mastering a large amount of material and information; for their judicious selection of the central and most cogent points; the clarity and readability of the exposition; the major effort and care with which they undertook their research and writing; the accuracy and clarity with which they reported their findings; and the authoritative guidance offered to the readers in understanding the complexity of the subject matter against the background of diverse cultures and settings. The book then offers a full report on the situation and application of the death penalty in India. The role and influence of different religions and politics on maintaining and applying the death penalty are addressed with considerable sensitivity and depth. The book then moves into a very important area that strongly influences continuing the death penalty's justification and application in the various regions of the world: public opinion. The authors and their team provide a very informative and well-summarized overview of public opinion in various parts of the world. This offers a unique panorama of the variety of viewpoints on this sensitive subject matter nuanced by the impact of different religious, cultural, and legal traditions. As the previous overview section, this part of the book constitutes a valuable summary of helpful perspectives and information of a global nature, an element especially important these days when globalization and instant communications impact all aspects of our lives and lead to a stronger awareness and also a growing convergence of laws, legal decisions, criminal justice practices, and standards of acceptable reactions to and punishment of crime.

The next section, chapter 5, delves into a delicate and profound aspect of the sentencing to and application of the death penalty: the psychosocial consequences that affect the victim of the crime being sanctioned and his/her family, the condemned's family, and those of others involved in the procedure from the jurors to the prison guards to the executioners. Then, the chapter examines some theoretical models used to explain the experiences of the victim's family in death penalty cases. Examples of models discussed are grief theory, PTSD, and the concept of closure. This literature survey offers a synopsis of very useful and current information that no doubt will be quite useful to anyone in the justice system and also in the therapeutic professions offering the victim's family their support and assistance.

The volume then delves into the key point: Public opinion in India. Chapter 6 constitutes the key contribution and the core value of this book. It is based on a survey with 25, 210 participants that were asked to respond to a questionnaire especially developed for this study. Since the support of public opinion is key to the perceived legitimacy and validity of the imposition and carrying out of the execution of the condemned, this chapter represents an original contribution to the public and legal discourse in India on the death penalty. It is a chapter rich in information, data, and nuanced analysis, providing a picture of the status of this key question in India. Reading it will offer a contemporary snapshot of where Indian public opinion is and of the reasoning, where values, religious influences, and personal understandings are in relation to this controversial theme. Thus, the contribution of this book to the dialogue on the death penalty in India is firmly anchored in empirical data and in its accurate analysis that takes into account the rich tapestry of Indian culture, laws, religions, and traditions.

The data are presented in a readily understandable manner with illustrations and tables easy to follow and capture. The conclusion of the study is that in India the death penalty has strong support across various strata of society.

In conclusion, this is an important work that provides a credible empirical basis for an informed debate in India about the death penalty against the rich backdrop of the global understanding and acceptance or not of this form of punishment and the universal call for recognition and respect of human life and truly impartial justice. It will no doubt enrich and guide the continuing debate on the issue and act as a reliable compass guiding it and helping maintain it in the realm of rationality in order to obtain a reasonable, credible, and well-founded outcome.

Prof. Emilio C. Viano
President
International Society of Criminology
Rome, Italy

American University
Washington, DC, USA

Advanced Accolades

Prof. **Andrew Taggart**
Emeritus Professor
Murdoch University

Dr. Sahni addresses an important topic that needs to be regularly critiqued, debated, and in fact resolved. The strong research base, with much needed contextual foci, should enable both the casual reader and the informed scholar to grow their personal and academic understandings of this divisive issue. The book and the large survey that underpins the findings explain in part why India sadly continues to allow the death penalty. Conclusions made, one hopes, may lead to the eventual end to the death penalty of the reluctant superpower, and I am thankful for this tome's publication.

Prof. Chee Ng
Healthscope Chair of Psychiatry
The Melbourne Clinic
Department of Psychiatry
University of Melbourne
Victoria

Congratulations on your forthcoming new book which contains the results of the survey of the general public in India on the death penalty. The findings would raise important public debate in the civil society on this global issue.

Prof. D.K. Srivastava
Formerly: Professor
City University of Hong Kong

Pro Vice-Chancellor and
Visiting Professor
O. P. Jindal Global University

This book by Dr. Sanjeev P. Sahni, an eminent professor and scholar, is an outstanding contribution to the understanding of the complicated issue like the death penalty. Dr. Sahni's empirical study based on public opinion of over 25,000 Indians on death penalty is a holistic work that discusses international rules, practices, human rights, and the psychological factors at play.

Dr. Sahni writes with enthusiasm and from an interdisciplinary perspective. The book has been enriched by his deep learning and expertise and will be welcomed by scholars and students of criminal justice system and constitutional law as well as human rights advocates in India and abroad.

Prof. (Dr.) Eduard Ivanov
National Research University
Higher School of Economics
Moscow, Russia

In twenty-first century, the application of death penalty is still a hot topic for discussion in many countries. Terrorist attacks, murders, and other cruel crimes bring part of the society to the idea that death penalty could be an effective measure to prevent these types of crime. Another part of the society has a completely different opinion. The book of Prof. Sahni on "The Death Penalty - Perspectives in India and Beyond" is a result of the solid academic study and a great contribution to the public discussion on death penalty.

Prof. (Dr.) G.S. Bajpai
Criminology & Criminal Justice
National Law University, Delhi

Eclectic and nonpareil, this book attempts to untangle a seminal paradox in death penalty scholarship as to why there is an inverse relationship between global efforts in the direction of abolition of death penalty and substantial opinions of the public regarding its effectiveness. The value of this work lies in its ability to map useful public perceptions on the practice of death penalty in India. It also leaves a question for the state to ponder over the emerging public concerns and a demand for harsher punishment at a time when criminal laws are expected to be more restorative and reparative.

Prof. Dr Hab. Dr H. C. Emil W. Pływaczewski
Dean (2012–2019) and Director of Institute of Criminal Law and Criminology - Faculty of Law University of Białystok, Poland

Member of The Stockholm Prize in Criminology Jury - Stockholm University, Sweden

As in any other society, there have emerged in India a number of popular, sometimes stereotypical views on capital punishment. These views are often expressed not just by the population at large but also by well-educated people.

So, it was a great idea to undertake a public opinion poll study for Indians on Death Penalty and document its results in this book. The research has shown that demographic variables are related to death penalty opinions due to attitudinal variables that underline them. In my opinion, the book of Professor Sahni is an excellent contribution for furthering the debate on the issue of capital punishment in India.

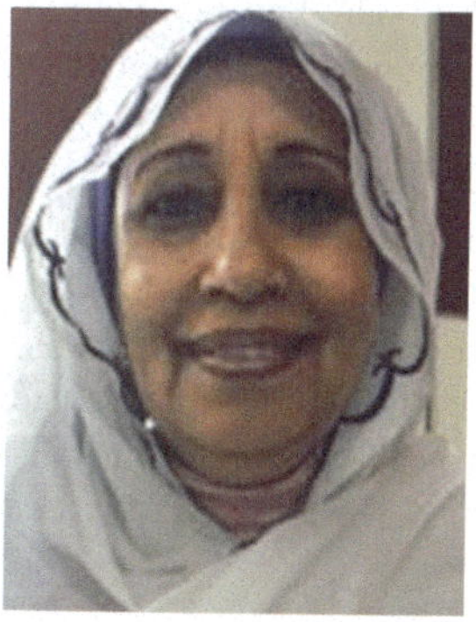

Ibtisam Satti Ibrahim Idris
University of Khartoum, Sudan

Put yourself in the shoes of the offender while you are reading, I am sure you will change your mindset.

Prof. (Dr.) Marc Groenhuijsen
Tilburg Law School
Professor, Department of Criminal Law & Professor at INTERVICT

Former President
World Society of Victimology
Tilburg, Netherlands

Dr. Sahni and his colleagues have once again produced a book that provides invaluable information on the entire scope of opinions among the Indian population about the imposition of the death penalty. This is compulsory reading for any expert in the field, since it offers a unique opportunity to compare the views of Indian citizens with the empirical criminological findings that have been collected all over the world during the past decade. Highly recommended!

Prof. Maria Stoicheva
Jean Monnet Chair
Sofia, Bulgaria

This book is a very valuable contribution to the worldwide perspective on death penalty. It is an enormously rich and highly penetrating study on understanding the perspective of general public in India on death penalty, its realities, and human rights issues involved. It provokes thought and offers insights on the weight that should be put on popular opinion, with an intellectually stimulating breadth relevant to considering the ambiguity and controversy over the abolition of capital punishment.

Michael O'Connell
Consulting Victimologist
Secretary-General
World Society of Victimology
Victim Advocate, Second Chances
SA Member, International Network Supporting Victims of Terrorism & Mass Violence (INVICTM)
Foundation & Board Member, Victim Support Asia (VSA)
Member, NGO Alliance on Crime Prevention & Criminal Justice
White Ribbon Ambassador
Australia Day Ambassador
Patron, Love Hope & Gratitude

In many countries, including India, the taking of life is a legal punishment. Considering, among other factors, the brutality of the death penalty, India's courts have ruled that the mandatory death penalty is unconstitutional. Notwithstanding, as Prof. Dr. Sanjeev Sahni's book reveals, the death penalty is deeply rooted in cultural and religious tenets across India.

Evaluating the death penalty from a victimological perspective is challenging and complex. Yet, Prof. Dr. Sahni's analysis of data attained from surveys of residents of India is wise, albeit by his own admission constrained. His book intelligently enriches the debate on the death penalty—a grotesque penalty that is acutely troubling.

Prof. Md. Ashraful Alam
Associate Professor
Department of Criminology and Police Science
Mawlana Bhashani Science and Technology University
Bangladesh

I believe this book by Prof. Dr. Sahni will contribute to draw a comparative and comprehensive picture about death penalty in the Indian subcontinent. It is very important that a large number of people participated with this research (25,210) and a significant number of participants (54.1% and 47%, respectively) believed that death penalty violates the right to life and is inhumane. In relation to the findings of the book, I also believe in Mahatma Gandhi's statement "I cannot in all conscience agree to anyone being sent to the gallows. God alone can take life because he alone gives it."

Congratulations to Dr. Sahni and his team for their efforts and patience in completing the research and publishing of this extraordinary book.

Prof. (Dr.) Nedjo Danilovic
President, International Association of Social Science Methodologists
Union University
Nikola Tesla, Belgrade

Professor Sanjev P. Sahni's book is dedicated to the scientific analysis of the views of the Indian public on the death penalty and its prospects, both in India and broader internationally. From an epistemological standpoint, the book is an extremely valuable monographic study that makes a significant contribution to the theory of socio-psychological and socio-criminological sciences, not only in India, but more broadly globally.

The scientific contribution of this monographic study is reflected in the authors' original scientific knowledge of the death penalty, and the remarkable social contribution is compounded by the practical possibilities of applying that knowledge to future Indian and world socio-psychological and criminological social practices.

Dr. Rico Sneller
Leiden University
Technical University Eindhoven

How thrilling to read a study about death penalty in a country where death seems to always be around the corner, not only for the poor and socially disadvantaged, that is, but also for those living in religiously and culturally explosive areas. What is more, India's rich spiritual tradition entails attitudes proclaiming life as sacrosanct. One wonders if these attitudes are strong enough to influence the average mentality of the people as regards death penalty. This study sheds a fascinating light on different Indian citizens' views of a form of punishment that is more and more under critique on a global scale.

Prof. (Dr.) Robert Peacock
President of the World Society of Victimology

Within a comparative and contextually sensitive framework, historically, socio-legally, culturally, and otherwise, this work presents with pioneering analyses of the crucial relationship between public opinion and punishment, and in particular perceptions in India on the perceived appropriateness and value of the Death Penalty. With a very impressive sample size critical analysis, the book generates an advanced and sophisticated understanding of the sensitivities surrounding this critical issue. This thoughtful study is mindful of background and mediating variables that could possibly influence public perceptions and provides therefore a benchmark and blueprint for future critical studies, particularly with reference to the arbitrary, final, and irrevocable nature of this form of punishment.

Prof. Scott Thompson-Whiteside
Pro Vice-Chancellor
Faculty of Health, Arts and Design
Swinburne University of Technology
Melbourne, Australia

Congratulations on your book contract and I am looking forward to hearing more about it when it is published.

Prof. (Dr.) Sima Avramović
University of Belgrade
Faculty of Law

To write a book about eternal topic of death penalty issues is always an immense challenge. Prof. Sanjeev Sahni has given a very interesting and important historical overview of the issue in ancient India, analyzed a lot of pros and cons of death penalty from societal and professional point of view, and offered an important contribution to the topic by organizing a huge public opinion poll with tens of thousands of participants. The results are not so unexpected, but it is important to have a scholarly proof of expectation that a great majority of the population in India are supporters of death penalty. Congratulations!

Virendra Sharma M.P.
UK

An important study that we needed of existing attitudes to the death penalty in India. As a strong supporter of abolition, I am pleased to better understand what drives public perception and opinion of the death penalty in India. Professor Sahni has shown again his stature as a behavioral scientist and I am thankful for this tome's publication.

Prof. Wu Hongyao
Professor of Law at the
China University of Political

Death penalty is not only a political decision, but also a historical and cultural matter. Professor Sanjeev's new book encompasses a comprehensive study about the death penalty in India by placing the status quo of India under the global context. The highlight of the book is the Indian public opinion poll study with respect to death penalty, which illustrates the public perception toward death penalty by spreading the poll among all age group. The poll is followed by an intrinsic analysis from psychosocial perspective. This book will contribute to the global justice by providing a new and inspiring research angle.

Prof. Dr. Dr. h. c. Miguel Abel Souto
President of the Ibero-American Association of Economic and Business Criminal Law

Professor of Criminal Law
University of Santiago de
Compostela, Spain

This book is an intelligent, talented, mature, and very interesting research about death penalty.

It is true that "demographic variables are related to death penalty opinions," but science needs rational arguments. In my opinion, according to Bockelmann (1962, p. 139), the most important rational argument against the death penalty is that there is no rational argument in its favor.

I invite you to read and enjoy this fascinating, impressive, magnificent, and valuable book.

Prof. Sam Garkawe
Professor of Law
Jindal Global Law School
O. P. Jindal Global University
Sonipat, India

Adjunct Associate Professor
School of Law and Justice
Southern Cross University
Lismore, Australia

Life Member of the
World Society of Victimology.

The election of populist governments around the world in recent times has shown that, if anything, there is a large gap between public opinion and the views of many decision-makers, professionals, and academics. Such people tend to take a liberal view on most issues. The issue of the death penalty and its relationship to the role of public opinion is an excellent example of this gap, and for this reason this book is both timely and thought-provoking. Notwithstanding the importance of the specific question of the death penalty, the book clearly has broader implications in the politics of today's world.

Preface

This book is an intrinsic piece of research on understanding the perspective of general public in India on "Death Penalty." Leading organizations like United Nations, Amnesty International are supporting the abolishment movement. Amnesty International reports that more than two-third of all countries in the world have abolished death penalty in law or in practice, although a few have subsequently reintroduced it. The parallel adoption and signature to international instrument on this subject pronounced that no one should be deprived of life.

Death penalty is retained for "rarest of the rare" crime events in India. The provisions and codes to justify judicial executions date back to ancient Indian literature like Kautilya Arthashatra. The book draws attention on crucial position of public of India on the issue of Death Penalty. It has been noticed worldwide that general public opinion differs from the worldwide movement favoring abolishment. In several countries, death penalty has been defended on grounds of public support. The present study was a public opinion poll of Indians with respect to death penalty. The main objective of the study was to understand their perception toward death penalty, reasons for support/opposition, type of crime for which death penalty is supported, and demographic factors associated with public opinion on death penalty. About 25210 Indians participated in the current study. They were in the age group of 12–80 years ($M_{Age} = 29.76$, $SD = 12.63$). Majority of the participants supported (80%) for death penalty primarily for crimes such as rape (77.7%) and murder (64%). Those favoring death penalty believed that it is proportionate to the wrong done (43.1%) and has a deterrence effect (39.1%) while those who opposed death penalty believed that it violates the right to life (54.1%) and is inhumane (47.4%). The results imply that public perception is in support of death penalty particularly when atrocious crimes are involved even though it is highly subjective. Some participants also believed that a systematic nature of death penalty may play a deterrent role, at least in some cases.

The book addresses the diverse sensitivities on death penalty through seven chapters citing the Global context, Indian context, role of non-state actors, public opinion poll on death penalty, psychosocial factors affecting death penalty, Indian perception on death penalty, and way forward. Each chapter critically reviews and draws conclusion on the topic addressed.

Sonipat, India

Sanjeev P. Sahni
Mohita Junnarkar

Acknowledgements

The book has evolved out of a research study to understand the perception of Indians toward Death Penalty. The book draws attention on crucial position of Indians on the issue of Death Penalty. The study was conducted in 25 states and 4 union territories of India. The results indicated that public perception is in support of death penalty particularly when atrocious crimes are involved even though it is highly subjective. Some participants also believed that a systematic nature of death penalty may play a deterrent role. This study commenced due to inspiration of distinguished Prof. Roger Hood, an authority in the area of Death Penalty from Oxford University.

We would like to take this opportunity to express our immense gratitude to Mr. Naveen Jindal, Founding Chancellor of O. P. Jindal Global University. He has not only provided excellent academic ambience but is highly supportive of all research initiatives. Without his encouragement, this study would not have seen the light of the day.

Our earnest and heartfelt thanks to our Vice-Chancellor, Professor C. Raj Kumar for his unstinted continuous encouragement to Jindal Institute of Behavioral Sciences (JIBS) to undertake research on "Death Penalty: A Public Opinion Poll". He was also instrumental in introducing Dr. Sahni to Prof. Roger Hood at Oxford University. The inspiration and motivation bestowed by Dr. Hood laid the guiding path for this book.

We would like to appreciate and thank Prof. Garima Jain, Assistant Professor at JIBS who helped to conceptualize the project on Death Penalty through her scientific acumen and also assisted in data collection and analysis.

The contribution of JIBS Research Fellows (Ms. Sweta Lakhani, Ms. Aishwarya Thakur, Ms. Vartika Srivastava, and Ms. Tanni Choudhary) and JGLS students (Mr. Manan Shishodia, Ms. Disha, and Mr. Vineet Sawant) was outstanding. They helped to formulate the initial drafts of the book. We are thankful to Mr. Hanan Zaffar who assisted in the final editing of the book.

The book would not have seen the current day of light without contribution of Prof. (Dr.) Jagdish Batra who edited the book meticulously. We express our heartfelt gratitude to Mr. Raj Revri, Ex-Diplomat, Ministry of External Affairs, Government of India for the insightful suggestions and reviewing the book.

We are also thankful to the administrative staff at Jindal Institute of Behavioral Sciences who helped us with data entry and other administrative tasks for the completion of the book.

Lastly, but definitely not the least, we are indebted to our family members who provided us with the strength and motivation. It was their unconditional love, care, and tolerance which made this book writing process smoother.

Contents

About the Authors

Prof. (Dr.) Sanjeev P. Sahni is the Professor and Principal Director of the Jindal Institute of Behavioural Sciences (JIBS), Director for Center for Victimology and Psychological Sciences, Member of the Governing Body; and Advisor to the Vice Chancellor at O. P. Jindal Global University. He holds a PhD degree in Psychology and possesses an extensive and rich experience of 32 years in Academia, Industry and Government Sector. His work spans in the areas of organizational behavior, criminal psychology, cognitive and neuropsychology, forensic psychology and policing and law enforcement. He has trained over 32000 Professionals in over 50 countries. He has served and contributed 14 years as a Scientist in the Ministry of Human Resource Development and Sports Authority of India. He has also served as Head- Human Resources at the Jindal Group. He has worked as a Research Scientist at several Universities like University of Houston, Texas; University of Illinois, Chicago to name a few. Dr. Sahni has been a guest faculty since 2017 at China University of Political Science and Law (CUPL) to teach Criminal Psychology. Dr. Sahni has several awards to his credit, and has recently been nominated as a Member of the Board of Directors of the International Society of Criminology. He is also a UN liaison committee member of World Society of Victimology (WSV). Among his several academic endeavours he has been regularly representing India at United Nations Office on Drugs and Crime (UNODC – Austria, Doha, Japan) and Academic Council on the United Nations System (ACUNS – South Africa). He has published more than 30 research articles in International and National Indexed Journals, and about 20 book chapters. With 14 Books to his credit, some of the recent ones are Internet Infidelity (Springer), Digital Piracy in the Digital Era (Springer), Crime And Criminal Law Perspectives On Global Migration(Har-Anand), Refugee Jurisprudence And Criminal Justice (Har-Anand), Conflict: The Police and The People (Lexis Nexis) and Global Perspectives of Victimology and Criminology (Bloomsbury).

Dr. Mohita Junnarkar currently working as Assistant Professor and Deputy Director at Jindal Institute of Behavioural Sciences, O. P. Jindal Global University, Sonipat, Haryana and has about 6 years of experience in research and teaching. Her research interests are applied positive psychology, psychometrics, cognitive psychology and adolescent development. She has to her credit about 20 papers in peer-reviewed international and national journals, 3 books, and 8 books chapters. She has published books in area of psychometric and positive psychology (Measures in Positive Psychology: Development and Validation, Springer), and behavioural sciences (Maximizing Human Potential through Behavioural Competencies: 100 Core Competencies, Bloomsbury; Child Adoption: A Study of Adopted Adolescents, Lambert Academic Publishing). She has also presented over 20 papers at national and international conferences. She has been teaching courses in cognitive and positive psychology and psychometrics at various public and private universities. She is also one of the founding team members of National Positive Psychology Association and is the reviewer for the Journal of the Indian Academy of Applied Psychology. Currently she is serving as the Founding President for the International Association of Young Psychologists.

List of Figures

List of Tables

Chapter 1
Death Penalty: A Global Context

The death penalty is like no other punishment. Its continued existence in the world creates political and civil tensions in many countries. The citizens of this world are divided in their stance on the capital punishment. The governments of the countries across continents can be divided into two categories—those that are retentionists and others who are abolitionists. However, the world has come a long way and now capital punishment is considered just another kind of punishment prescribed by law. Although some people oppose it, the majority of the nations support it. The change came in the post-Second World War era, when crimes against humanity and barbaric methods of torture started being abolished and with it, countries also started abolishing this form of punishment. Gradually humane practices spread. Major reasons for this practice of abolition to gain recognition can be attributed to growth in human rights activism. Many international organizations and instruments were formed to protect human rights and a general awareness was being raised over the heinous nature of death penalty that has caused abolition of the capital punishment to rise. However, some major countries across the globe do not agree with the notion that capital punishment is a human rights issue and still retain the death penalty for certain crimes or in exceptional circumstances.

The following chapter will address the question and provide insight on what is the stance of countries across the globe while dealing with death penalty. The laws and regulations regarding the usage of death penalty spread throughout the globe. What made some countries still practice it, while others don't practice and how religious ideologies can also play a part in this. Using statistics collected from various sources and research into the laws and trends that countries follow, the author aims to provide a wholesome global view with regard to the status of death penalty.

The Rule of Law, as proposed first by A. V. Dicey over a century ago, suggests that the law of the land is supreme (Principe, 2000). Every citizen is subjected to such laws and violation of such laws cannot be done without any legal repercussion and liability. With the passage of time, there have been numerous debates and criticism of this theory but the basic principle still stands. The law of the land can curtail rights if there has been a violation of someone else's right which disrupts the public order of the state while right to life is no exception.

S. P. Sahni and M. Junnarkar, *The Death Penalty*,
https://doi.org/10.1007/978-981-15-3129-3_1

The Constitutions of countries around the world acknowledge the Right to Life. This right is a fundamental right conferred upon citizens by their respective country's framework. The Constitution of The United States of America, 1789 guarantees right to life by the virtue of the 14th Amendment; Article 21 of the Constitution of India, 1950 confers right to life; Article 9(1) of the Constitution of the Republic of Singapore, 1965 confers this right and globally too when it comes to the three basic Human rights of a Person, Right to life is one of them by virtue of Article 3 of the Universal Declaration of Human Rights. Although the Right to Life is a person's inherent right but the conferment of such a right without any restrictions can only be termed as an idealistic view of the world.

Capital Punishment or death penalty is the most severe form of punishment prescribed in law which dictates that for the most severe crimes stipulated under the law, the convicts should be executed by a procedure laid down in the law of the land. The Capital punishment of death penalty is majorly given by countries across the globe for the most heinous crimes that can be committed by a person. The debate between the advocates that support capital punishment and those who condemn it has been going on since ages. Whether or not a convict should be sentenced to death is not just a matter of the law of the land, but it also entails a huge human rights issue. As stated in Article 3 of the Universal Declaration of Human Rights, right to life is guaranteed to any person just by the virtue of that person being a human being then how can any legal system allow taking of a human's life legally without any sanctions for a law enforcement state body? To this question, there are numerous answers and arguments to be made to support or oppose the notion of death penalty and such have been discussed in the coming chapters of this book. Religion can also be seen to play a huge part in the usage of the same. All the religions have their own views and methodologies on the subject of death penalty which are propagated by religious texts and rituals.

Currently, majority of the countries over the globe have abolished death penalty for all the crimes which include countries such as Guinea, Angola, Seychelles, and other such countries. But some of the major countries such as the United States of America, Singapore, Japan, and China do retain death penalty and continue to carry out executions. To explain further, the countries can be divided into four broad categories. First category is of countries that retain death penalty both in practice and law. A total of 54 countries out of the whole come under this category. Second category lists those countries that have abolished death penalty de facto, which means that they have abolished it as per the Amnesty International standards which dictate that such practices are not carried out or continued or perform execution and 30 countries are listed in this category who adhere to this. Third is that of those 7 countries that have abolished it de jure as well as de facto which means they have not conducted any execution in more than 14 years but still retain it on their books for special circumstances and exceptions such as against crimes committed in wartime. The last and fourth category is of 102 countries that have abolished it completely for all of the crimes, such as Fiji abolished it in 2015 and so did Republic of Congo and Madagascar. The most recent countries to join this category are Guinea and Mongolia in 2017 (Amnesty International, 2018).

As per the data that has been elaborated further in the coming chapters, the image one can draw is that the Governments and their legislatures of the world are divided in their stance when it comes to corporal punishment. To provide a global view of the legal status of corporal punishment, continentwise literature will be analyzed. The author will be adopting a continentwise approach to shed light upon the stance taken by different member states of different conventions and international law instruments which help to shape their legal provisions with regard to death penalty. The author will be tracing data and statistical reports collected through a pool of resources to analyze and discuss the global view of corporal punishment. The author will also discuss the relation between religious teachings and death penalty and how is it that religion professed by majority citizens of a nation affects the legal status of corporal punishment.

1.1 African Continent

In the African continent, out of the 54 states that are members to the United Nations charter, 20 states have abolished the capital punishment in their law of which 18 states do not execute those convicts who have been sentenced to death any longer. Therefore, a total 38 states out of the 54 can thus be termed as abolitionist states who have let go of the death penalty both in law and practice. The remaining 16 states still retained the death penalty as a punishment (World Coalition Against Death Penalty, n.d.).

The continent of Africa has been seen as a "Ray of Hope" for all the advocates of the abolition of Death penalty due to the fact that majority of countries in this continent have expressly abolished death penalty both in law and practice.

A significant number of executions were reduced by almost 49% in the region in 2016. There were only 22 executions recorded in 2016 compared to 43 in 2015. Guinea abolished death penalty for all crimes whereas Burkina Faso, Gambia, and Kenya have taken important steps toward abolishing death penalty. In January 2016, the Constitutional Court of Benin ruled that "*in order to comply with the country's international human rights obligations, all laws providing for the death penalty were void and death sentences could no longer be imposed in the country*". The landmark decision effectively abolished the death penalty in the country. The reason behind this was the following of the trend set by Madagascar and Republic of Congo in 2015. The Sub-Saharan Africa has shown firm and favorable pace toward abolishment of death penalty. Back in 1977 when Amnesty International had just started out to campaign worldwide for the abolition of the death penalty, no country in Sub-Saharan Africa accepted this practice of abolishment of the death penalty for all crimes but what can be described as a drastic change, 19 in the continent have accepted the suggestion (Popoola, 2017). In North African part of the continent, Tunisia has been execution free since 1991 and is one of the first countries in the region to adopt this practice. Although no official moratorium exists to be in force yet there is a settled policy to not conduct executions in the state of Morocco which has been execution free since the year 1993.

In South Africa, what is also known as the "Cape of Good Hope", death penalty has been abolished since 23 years now. In 1995, at a time when the Supreme Court of South Africa was newly constituted and few landmark judgements had been passed, this judgement came as a breath of fresh air for the general population. During the 1980s, there was a rapid increase seen in executions. The pro-execution government at the time had already executed 164 people in 1987 alone. This number is still known as the highest in any other country. Of the 2949 hangings performed since 1959, 1123 were in the 80s of which 14 were women (Snyman, 2018). Till the time the death penalty was abolished, it had been implemented not only for murder but also for crimes such as rape, housebreaking and robbery or attempted robbery with aggravating circumstances, sabotage, training abroad to further the aims of communism, kidnapping, terrorism, and treason. It had been a mandatory punishment until courts got the power to impose lesser sentences if they found circumstances to be extenuating. But the change of abolishment came from the Supreme Court case of State v Makwanyane and Mchunu, 1985 in which the apex court after hearing both sides ended up abolishing the death penalty and stated that "Everyone, including the most abominable of human beings, has a right to life, and capital punishment is therefore unconstitutional." (CCT3/94). However, the current debate that has been doing the rounds among the law-makers and the public of South Africa is whether the country needs the death penalty to be incorporated back in their legal system. In view of rise in crimes such as "aggravated robbery, which rose from 219 per 100,000 of population to 239 (by 9%), the number of aggravated robberies taking place each day has risen from 232 to 354 (by 52%)" (South African Institute of Race relations, 2016).

However, in Algeria due to the conflicts in the region over the past years, the amount of crimes including heinous crimes has increased and in response to this ever growing crime rate, more serious forms of punishment such as capital punishment have also risen (Report of Human Rights Committee, General Assembly, 1998). The chairman of the National Advisory Commission for the Protection and Promotion of Human Rights in 2016 announced that Algeria intended to abolish capital punishment. But, just a month later, Algeria's new criminal code which includes references to death penalty was given the green signal by the council of ministers and it still does contain references to the death penalty (Hood & Hoyle, 1996a, b, c, d, e).

Egypt remains one of the states to adopt the usage of the death penalty for crimes such as murder, rape as well as offences related to drug trafficking. An amendment made to the country's penal code in 1992 saw death penalty being extended to "terrorist offences" and as a derivative of this action, the country saw a huge rise in the number of convictions leading to death sentences from 21 to 108 over the span of 7 years (Amnesty International, 2000; Amnesty International, 2001; Amnesty International, Egypt, 2002).

When it comes to the Sub-Saharan Africa, there has been an emerging trend which has caused circumstances to get heated up. Upon taking statistics into account, it has been noticed that ever since last year, the region has seen a rapid increase in the number of death sentences being pronounced which is a surprise because overall the number of countries where death sentences were imposed by the Courts has actually dipped from 21 in 2015 to 17 in 2016. There has been an explosive 145% increase in the number of death sentences imposed across the region and in comparison to 443 sentences in 2015, the number has gone up to 1,086 death sentences which were confirmed in 2016 (Popoola, 2017). This sharp increase in the numbers can be attributed directly to a massive surge in Nigeria where the courts imposed the highest number of death sentences in Africa with a total of 527 death sentences. "*This high number of death sentences in Nigeria raises serious concerns about the real possibility of executing the innocent, as unsafe convictions are common. In fact, the courts in the country exonerated 32 wrongly convicted people in 2016 alone*" (Popoola, 2017).

A monumental shift for Kenya and its people came on December 14, 2017 when the long-standing law on mandatory death penalty was declared unconstitutional by the Supreme Court of Kenya in a historic decision. Prior to this, section 204 of the penal code of Kenya did not provide any discretionary power to the judges to consider mitigating circumstances that led to the crime, rather the law provided for automatic death penalty being awarded if convicted for crimes like murder, treason, and armed robbery. The abolition of the mandatory death penalty is another step taken by Kenya to show its unwillingness to support the death penalty. Indeed, with no executions since 1987, Kenya comes under the ambit of a de facto abolitionist country (World Coalition Against Death Penalty, 2018).

1.2 American Continent

In the American continent, out of 35 independent American states, which are signatories to the United Nations Charter, 37% of these states maintain death penalty both in law and practice; 14% of these states allow death penalty but only restricted to exceptional circumstances such as wartime; 3% of these states have not used it in the period of 10 years although it is permissible under there law; and finally, 46% of the states have completely abolished it (Cornell Center on the Death Penalty Worldwide, n.d.).

The United States of America remains unclear regarding the stance of exercising capital punishment upon convicts. The concept of capital punishment does exist in 31 states out of the 50 states whereas 19 of them have abolished it completely from their legal system due to deterrence promulgated by the recent debates and change in the ideology of the justice system (Death Penalty Database, Cornell Center on the Death Penalty Worldwide). As per the current prevailing federal law, each state has the authority to impose a death penalty for murders involving actions or situations that are usually referred to as special circumstances and at the same time, every state has full authority and power to also ban the death penalty (Gracetti, 2014). The shift in the ideology that has been growing in the United States is that of imposing a countrywide ban on the practice of the death penalty and replacing it with life imprisonment for the convicts who have been convicted for the heinous of crimes; however, this shift has not been rapid among all the states. The advocates who are against the idea of capital punishments such as human rights activist have not only questioned the methods used in execution but also have deemed the methods as inhuman and condemned them for gross violation of human rights of the inmates.

In the state of California, a long-term battle has been going on since the reinstatement of death penalty after the voters opted for it in 1978. But in the coming years, this support of the voters saw a continuous decline due to the improper implementation and questionable procedures that were used to carry out the executions. In 2004, the California State Senate established a bipartisan blue-ribbon panel named as California Commission on the Fair Administration of Justice. The panel was tasked with (i) speeding up the death penalty process, (ii) investigating the causes of wrongful convictions, (iii) investigating the executions in the state, and (iv) recommending reforms (Gracetti, 2014). However, there was a lack of meaningful change in the death penalty legislature that was finally adopted after deliberations (Gracetti, 2014). However, a stand still in the process of administering lethal injections as a form of execution came from the Case of *Morales vs. Cullen, 2005*. During the proceedings, many objections were raised as to the constitutional validity of usage of lethal injection being given to a convict under the eighth amendment of the United States Constitution. The Eighth Amendment of 1791 to the United States Constitution states: "Excessive bail shall not be required, nor excessive fines imposed, nor cruel and unusual punishments inflicted." This amendment prohibits the federal government from imposing unduly harsh penalties on criminal defendants, either as the price for obtaining pretrial release or as punishment for crime after conviction. The following year, that is in 2006, the case of *Pacific News Service v. Cullen, 2006* was being adjudicated. It was a challenge raised by an inmate against the use of a paralytic drug in lethal injection. The arguments put forth by the inmate were that the usage of this paralytic drug in execution was in violation of the First Amendment rights. The First Amendment prevented the press and the public from witnessing the execution procedures, primarily, due to two reasons: (i) First Amendment and (ii) shortage of lethal injection drugs. All the legal cases that invited death penalty were placed on indefinite hold. The last execution in California occurred in 2006 (Gracetti, 2014). Ever since that last execution, the state of California has retained the death penalty in law but not in practice.

In a broader view of the overall status since decades regarding capital punishment throughout the United States of America, since 1976, 14 out of all the retentionist states have executed no more than six people. In fact, since 1977, 83% of all executions have been carried out in just nine states, namely, Texas, Virginia, Oklahoma, Missouri, North and South Carolina, Georgia, Alabama, and Florida. Out of these, maximum of the executions have been carried out in Texas alone. Death Sentences fell from 317 in 1996 to 114 in 2006 and executions from 98 in 1999 to 53 in 2006. Between 2001 and 2006, just 21 of the 38 states with death penalty carried out an execution. The 53 executions in 2006 occurred primarily in 14 states in which Texas has carried out 24 of these, Ohio conducted five and Florida, North Carolina, Virginia,

Oklahoma carrying out four executions each. Another statistic to ponder upon is that in the year 2006, 69% of all the states in the United States carried out no executions at all and out of these, there are 14 states which have abolished the punishment but also the percentage is inclusive of the 22 states which did have the statute in their respective laws but still did not carry out any execution (Hood & Hoyle, 1996a, b, c, d, e).

In Canada, the death penalty can be traced back to as far as 1859, where all the executions in Canada were conducted by hanging, which was the method commonly adopted in matter where civilians were convicted or shooting in those matters where military personnel were to be executed. However, there was a constant notion of abolishment of death penalty floating in the Canadian scenario due to ideals of their political leaders. It was in 1967 when there was an official moratorium placed on the usage of death penalty but the formal abolishment came in the year 1976 by virtue of amendments made to the Criminal Code, when the House of Commons narrowly passed Bill C-84. By then, Canada had hanged 710 people since capital punishment was enacted in 1859. It was only in 1998 that Canada wiped out all references to capital punishment, with its elimination from the National Defence Act for such military offences such as treason and mutiny (Death Penalty in Canada, Amnesty International).

Shifting the focus toward the Caribbean, Barbados emerges as a country which practices abolitionist de facto, which means that although there is nothing in the statutory law stating that death penalty is executed by way of a hanging, however the source can be traced back to the reservations that have been made by Barbados to the American convention (Death penalty and executions in 2017, Amnesty International). The American convention of human rights was brought into existence from 1969 but has been effective since July, 1978. Under this convention, Barbados has reserved its right to execute death penalty by way of hanging for the commission of treason and murder. It is interesting to see that under International Law, by way of reservations, signatory states create exceptions for their own self which does contradict the objective of the convention but nevertheless, is allowed owing to the sovereign nature of a state to make their own laws. The trend of nation states becoming abolitionist of death penalty under such instruments however reserving the right to use exceptions in certain situations can be seen as a compromise being struck by such states. On one hand, major use of death penalty does get abolished but on the other hand, the state does hold the penalty in case of heinous crimes.

1.3 Asian Pacific Continent

In the region of Asia-Pacific, out of the 57 United Nations members states, 44% of these maintain death penalty both in law and practice; 3% of these states allow death penalty but only restricted to exceptional circumstances such as wartime; 16% of these states have not used it in the period of 10 years although it is permissible under their law; 37% of the states have completely abolished it. Of the 41 countries in Asia and the Pacific, 13 are retentionist, 1 is abolitionist for ordinary crimes, 10 are abolitionist in practice, 17 are abolitionist for all crimes, and 28 have abolished the death penalty in law and/or practice (Anti-Death Penalty Asia Network, n.d.).

The Asian continent has had a significant history that has not only shaped the present status of the countries but has also affected almost every country on the planet when considered from a global issue parameter. The problem of colonialism, economic and social backwardness, and most of all being termed as the third world nations has always in some way or the other kept the continent in an inferior light. These reasons have led to the significant growth that is seen today. Countries like China, India, Singapore, and many others have risen in the ranks of the world leaders to realize their power and importance in world issues. With regard to this, a Charter document in 1998 was formed with the help of over 200 NGOs in order to provide soft law principles to be adopted to fulfill international human rights obligations. The preamble itself is a testament to their aim. The preamble states "For long, especially during the colonial period, the peoples of Asia suffered from gross violations of their rights and freedoms. Today, large sections of our people continue to be exploited and oppressed and many of our societies are torn apart by hatred and intolerance. Increasingly the people realize that peace and dignity are possible only when the equal and inalienable rights of all persons and groups are recognized and protected. They are determined to secure peace and justice for themselves and the coming generations through the struggle for human rights and freedoms. Toward that end, they adopt this Charter as an affirmation of the desire and aspirations of the peoples of Asia to live in peace and dignity" (Asian Human Rights Charter, 1998). In this Charter, under right to life, Article 3.7 lays down the condition that all the states party to this charter must abolish the death penalty. If and where the penalty exists, it may be imposed only for the rarest of rare crimes. A convict must be given an opportunity of a fair trial before an independent and impartial tribunal with full and reasonable opportunity of "legal representation of his or her choice, adequate time for preparation of defence, presumption of innocence and the right to review by a higher tribunal. Execution should never be carried out in public or otherwise exhibited in public." (Asian Human Rights Charter, 1998). This charter, although has not been adopted by all the states of the continent, still shows the intent of human rights activists and advocates and even some states to abolish the death penalty regime in law. Another continentwide launch to abolish capital punishment was made on October 10th, 2006 by the name of Anti-Death Penalty Asia Network or ADPAN. It is a regional network of organization and individual members who work to establish abolition of death penalty all over the continent.

Currently in the Asia-pacific region, 17 countries such as Australia, Bhutan, and New Zealand have abolished it for all crimes whereas Fiji has just abolished death penalty for ordinary crimes and has retained it as punishment for heinous crimes that are more serious. Whereas there are 10 countries such as Brunei, Maldives, and Sri Lanka, which come under the category of those states that do retain death penalty for crimes such as murder/culpable homicide but some states are termed as abolitionist due to their practice of not carrying out any executions in the span of a decade whereas some have made a commitment to not carry out capital punishment (Anti-Death Penalty Asia Network, n.d.).

In countries such as Sri Lanka and Maldives, Buddhism as a religion is very prevalent. This prevalence and its effect can also be seen in their approach toward the death penalty. Buddhism, as per its teachings strongly opposes the death penalty. According to Buddhism, "The way to restore a wrong is not through another wrong. Rather, a counterweight is needed, so that the more evil there is on the one side, the more good there is on the other side. Buddhists believe in the cycle of birth and rebirth, Samsara, and that the death penalty will negatively affect the souls, the one who is punished and the one who punishes. Trying to gain recompense for evil, even violent death, by inflicting further death will simply cause a greater imbalance in the world; only rehabilitation has a chance to restore the harmony in life" (Marazziti, 2014a, b). Yet in states such as Thailand and Japan, death penalty is legal and is practiced.

China has been the center of scrutiny by activists and human rights advocates for being one of the countries with the most number of executions in the current times. The Secretary-General of Amnesty International, Salil Shetty states that "China wants to be a leader on the world stage, but when it comes to the death penalty it is leading in the worst possible way—executing more people annually than any other country in the world" (Amnesty International, 2017). China's Criminal Procedure Law of 1996 allows the use of lethal injections and shooting executions. However, by virtue of a verdict in 2009 by the People's Supreme Court, shooting executions have been discontinued. Shooting executions were discontinued in 2010 per a People's Supreme Court ruling of February 2009 which held that lethal injection is a more humane form of execution than shooting (Cornell Center on the Death Penalty Worldwide, n.d.). The process of lethal injection is carried out in prisons or in mobile "death vans," where prisoners are reportedly strapped to an electric-powered stretcher and injected with lethal drugs (Malone, 2009). China has also been accused of hiding the records of such executions by terming them as "State Secrets" and only show a tiny fraction of the actual amount of executions. Due to such allegations and constant investigations and reports from such investigations being conducted by acclaimed international bodies such as Amnesty International, pressure can be said to be on the government of China to make clarifications regarding their usage of death penalty and engage in dialog with such international bodies regarding their stance on this issue due to such alarming rate of executions by the state.

In the context of religion in India, Hinduism is practiced by a significant number of citizens across the country yet the views under Hinduism are fairly conflicting. The people who believe in death penalty and are supporters of it have adopted the reasoning of karma as stipulated in various religious texts and scriptures and believe that a person who commits wrong will get the same amount of wrong done to him by God in some other form. Whereas opposition of such views has adopted the view taken by Mahatma Gandhi himself that "take an eye for an eye and the whole world will be blind". However, when it is seen in connection with the laws in the state, this teaching is hardly followed.

In the light of laws and charters being established, the Indian stance on the subject is an imperative one. "Over the last forty years, there has been pressure in India to restrict the use of the death penalty, following a period between 1953 and 1963 when there had been at least 1,422 executions" (Hood & Hoyle, 1996a, b, c, d, e). Thus, it is safe to consider the gravity of the usage of this punishment to be severe in this state. In the judicial system, in 1980, the Judgement pronounced in the case of *Bachan Singh Vs. State of Punjab* is a Landmark Judgement as the question of constitutionality of the death penalty was addressed by the apex court of the country that is, the Supreme Court. While discussing the constitutionality in the case, the Supreme Court went on to state that "There are several other indications, also, in the Constitution which show that the Constitution-makers were fully cognizant of the existence of death penalty for murder and certain other offences in the Indian Penal Code and also, the mention in the legislative list, powers of the governor and the President to suspend, commute, or remit the death sentence and the power of appeal under Article 134 of the Constitution show that the death penalty or its execution cannot be regarded as unreasonable, cruel, or unusual punishment" (Bachan Singh v. State of Punjab, (1980) 2 SCC 684: 1980 SCC (Cri) 580 para 136).

Since then the concept of rarest of rare cases has been adopted by the Indian Judiciary and hence there has been a decline in the rate at which executions have been carried out. The cases of extreme brutality, gross murders, or mass killings have been seen to attract more of the pronouncement of death penalty in the state of India. Under the law, Murder is a punishable death offence under Article 302 of the Penal Code. For example, in case of armed robbery, if any one person commits murder, then all members of the group can be sentenced to death. Similarly, if a victim loses life after being kidnapped for ransom is too punishable by the death penalty. Death penalty can be awarded for other crimes such as (i) being a member of an association or promoting an association while committing any act using unlicensed firearms or explosives that results in death; (ii) engaging in organized crime and it results in death; (iii) committing or assisting another person in committing sati—the burning or burying alive of widows or women; (iv) bearing false witness in a capital case against a member of a scheduled caste or tribe, resulting in that person's conviction and execution, carries the death penalty (Under the Prevention of Atrocities Act). Furthermore, death penalty is also awarded for assisting individuals who are under the age of 18, mentally ill, mentally disabled, or intoxicated in committing suicide. However, in *Mithu v. State of Punjab*, the Supreme Court ruled that the mandatory death penalty is unconstitutional. While subsequent legislation for drug and atrocity offences prescribes the mandatory death penalty, and the Supreme Court has not expressly struck down the penalty as unconstitutional, Indian courts have not applied the mandatory death penalty for these crimes. Additionally, in a line of cases since the 1980 case of *Bachan Singh v. State of Punjab*, the Court held that the "death penalty should only be applied for the most heinous offences (the rarest of the rare)." (Cornell Center on the Death Penalty Worldwide, n.d.).

1.4 Middle East

The Quran (6:151) states "Take not life, which God has made sacred, except by way of justice and law." The Quran (5:32) states "Whoever slays a soul, unless it be for manslaughter or for mischief in the land, it is as though he slew all men; and whoever keeps it alive, it is as though he kept alive all men."

The above-stated injunctions taken from the Quran, which is the primary religious text for Islamic community show the stance toward death penalty. It propagates that a life can only be taken for justice through law and no wrong toward another human should be committed. Any wrong toward one human is a wrong committed toward the whole humanity. Thus, Islamic states such as Saudi Arabia do have strict laws conferring death penalty for crimes in order to provide strict deterrence for criminals. Saudi Arabia is ranked among the top three nations when it comes to carrying out executions coming after China and Iran according to Amnesty International's global death penalty report of 2014. Almost 2,208 people were executed between January 1985 and June 2015 and 102 people executed between January and June 2015. In the calendar year 2014, a total of 90 people got executed. As of 2015 "Out of the 48.5% of people that were executed between January 1985 and June 2015, 1,072 people were foreign nationals, who make up around 33% of Saudi Arabia's population of approximately 30 million. Executions for drug related offences rose from just 4% in 2010 and 2011 to 28% in 2012 and 32% in 2013. By 2014 and June 2015 the percentage had risen to 47%." (Amnesty International, 2015).

As for the period 2017–18, reports of similar trend of death penalty is seen. Saudi Arabia has been known to sentence prisoners to death even for minor offences. "Islamic law is derived from several sources. Primary guidance is obtained through Shari'a, the laws and ways of life prescribed by Allah. Shari'a is comprised of the Quran, considered to be Allah's direct words, and the Sunnah, the words and actions of the Prophet Muhammad." (Peiffer, 2005). Due to such un-codified sources of law, the usage of death penalty and other forms of serious punishment is more in these nations and is known to be one of the causes of such high rates of sentencing. Thus, it can be said that religious teachings and specially the words taken from Quran which speak about taking a person's life for justice and law is permissible and therefore, the impact can be clearly seen on the law practiced by the nation.

Same trend is seen in Iran as well. Iran has constantly, through the decades, been known to be a pro-execution country. The nation has carried out the most executions in the middle-east region in the year 2014. The following year by the end of the first half of the year, the government had already executed more than a total of some other nations put together. The number was nearly around 700 people and the major part of this number was not even officially acknowledged by the authorities.

Amnesty International lists the Iranian justice system as the second most prolific executioner in the world after China. The Iran Human Rights Documentation Center and Iran reported that the Islamic Republic of Iran had executed 64 of its own citizens in the first few weeks of January, 2015. Reportedly there are various grounds by virtue of which the government of Iran gives its justification for performance of death penalty as a method of punishment. According to the reports, the individuals who are convicted as offenders by the government are accused of having acted against the religious rules. Many such convicts are termed to be Moharebeh which translates to those who wage war against God. However, the majority of those who are executed are convicted on (i) simple drug charges, and (ii) practicing homosexual or blasphemy against Prophet Muhammad. Gay activists estimate that some 4,000 alleged gays have been executed by Iran since its 1979 Islamic Revolution (Death Sentences and Executions, Amnesty International). The famous execution of Mahmoud Asgari and Ayaz Marhoni in 2005 can be said to be a one of the hundred cases which have been reported of execution of people on the charge of being homosexual (Mixed Reports on Iran Teen Hanging, Greenberg). Iran also has the world's highest rate of execution by stoning. There is no official report available about the actual number of cases where executions have been carried out through stoning in Iran but according to an Iranian human rights lawyer, Shadi Sadr, there are at least 11 convicts who have died (Death Penalty in Middle East, International Centre of human Rights, 2017).

1.5 European Continent

In the European Continent, the statistics are quite contrary to those of the other continents. Ninety-six percent of these states have abolished death penalty. Only 4% of these allow death penalty, both in law and practice. It is a pre-condition to membership of the European Union that death penalty must be abolished from law and practice as the stance of the European Union is that the very concept of capital punishment is inhuman and thus directly in contravention of the human right to life. An exception here is that of Belarus. Belarus is the only country in the European continent to carry out executions of convicts since 1999 (Cornell Law School, 2012).

In the fight against death penalty, the European Union has repeatedly utilized their wide set of diplomatic and cooperation assistance tools, to name a few, like statements, demarches, and Human Rights Dialogs. "The EU continues to underline that the Death Penalty is of a cruel and inhumane character and it is incompatible with human dignity and the right to life. It is irreversible in case of miscarriage of justice; it does not deter crime more effectively than other punishments. Abolition of the death penalty does not lead to an increase in crime." (European Union External Action, n.d.). The fact that Europe is known as a "Death Penalty-Free Zone" is a result of such regulations imposed by the European Union. Membership to this union depends on whether the nation has abolished death penalty or not. This method of deterrence seems to be working, as currently majority of the nations are a death penalty-free zone.

One of the pioneering nations to abolish death penalty was Portugal in 1867 and as the twentieth century was dawning upon the world, the abolishing practice was followed by Italy and Republic of San Marino as well. In Germany, after the Holocaust and gross crimes which were committed against humanity, although pressure was there for retention, yet the Article 102 of the New Constitution of the Federal

Republic in 1949 expressly abolished capital punishment for all crimes, no matter what the circumstance (Evans, 1996). In 1918, Belgium carried out its last execution for murder but then death penalty was abolished for all offences officially in 1996 (Toussiant, 1999).

The United Kingdom has come a long way toward abolition of death penalty. Starting from 1810, by law, there were 223 offences for which one could be sentenced to death. However, out of those 939 convicts who were pronounced a death sentence, only 123 convicts were actually executed. Among the convicts who were executed in the year 1810, they were pronounced to death for committing various categories of crime. Some were convicted for burglary, some for forgery, and some for murder. What is astonishing is that people executed for burglary and forgery were more than the people executed for murder (Radzinowicz, 1948). Due to such disproportionate sentences being continuously imposed upon people who had committed far less serious crimes than the ones that actually carried severe punishments attached to them, many debates and arguments were led by jurists and advocates for urgent amendments so that this anomaly in law could be fixed. Soon, due to this movement and works of the "Criminal Law Commissioners", people argued for such amendments. In England and Wales, murder became the only crime for which executions were carried out. In 1861, crimes that had death penalty attached were treason, arson, and murder and for all other offences, usage of capital punishment was abolished (Hood & Hoyle, 1996a, b, c, d, e). The status of death penalty in the United Kingdom has gone through a lot of such debates and movements where many experiments were conducted to find a substitute for it in terms of life imprisonment. As a culmination of its history, the current stance is that after the last execution conducted in 1964, death penalty was abolished for murder in 1965 and for offences such as treason, piracy, and in military law in the year 1998. Further, on account of the 13th Protocol of the European Convention on Human Rights, the United Kingdom is bound to abolish death penalty for all offences.

Christianity as a religion has been attributed to contribute to this abolishment. Christians are one of the most active advocates for abolishment of the death penalty in law and practice due to their beliefs that life can only be taken by God and no authority has this sacred right. The view taken by Churches which support abolishment is that it directly flows from the Bible as life is considered as a gift from the Almighty and it is inhuman to have it taken away by any other human or authority even by law. The Bible cites references through verses to crimes punishable by death. However, the eminent eye-for-an-eye code ensured reduction of revenge and punishment from "seventy times seven" to a more proportionate measure (Marazziti, 2014a, b). The practice of death penalty abolishment in UK as being caused by the faiths of Christianity cannot be considered as a sound reasoning. It can be argued that such beliefs do affect the views of people but as stated above in this chapter, the public outrage over disproportionate sentencing is seen as the main reason for abolishment.

1.6 Conclusion

To draw a curtain on this chapter, different stances of different countries spread over the continents of the world have been laid down. The growing trend of moving away from the death penalty can be seen as an ongoing wind of change which is slowly but surely blowing over the globe. Countries such as those in the European continent with Portugal and Italy leading the way, some states in the United States of America—the major one being California which after series of legal cases has come to a stop along with Benin and Congo among others stated in this chapter—have succumbed to the need of human rights and moved away from the practice of death penalty. However, what is surprising is that emerging powerful nations of the world such as China, India, and Singapore have somehow reached all-time high rates of death penalty that history has ever seen. Religion does play a part in this process as the holy scriptures and ancient teachings do seem to affect the stance on death penalty of the nations but then again no clarity is present due to various conflicts in their own practice.

The question that beckons here is which stance should be favored? The countries where death penalties have been abolished can be said to adhere to the human rights obligations but on the other hand, the countries that retain death penalty do it by force of their internal law for crimes that are heinous that shock the humanity. If one goes by the trend in the global context it seems the nations of the world are moving toward a no death penalty future but recent statistics of a few nations and the uncertainty of actions of some states do seem to make this future a rather distant but not an impossible one.

References

Amnesty International. (2018). The death penalty in 2017 facts and figures, 12 April 2018.
Amnesty International, Report 2000 (p. 96); Amnesty International, Report 2001 (p. 92); Amnesty International, Egypt, Increasing Use of Death Penalty 2002, AI Index: MDE 12/017/2002.
Amnesty International, Report 2007 (p. 202).
Anti-Death Penalty Asia Network, Fact and figures, n.d.
Asian Human Rights Charter 1998.
Bachan Singh v. State of Punjab, (1980) 2 SCC 684: 1980 SCC (Cri) 580 para 136.
Death Penalty: World's Biggest Executioner China must come clean about 'Grotesque' level of capital punishment, Amnesty International, 2017.
Death Sentences and Executions, Amnesty International, 2014.
Death Penalty Database, Cornell Center on the Death Penalty Worldwide, n.d.
Death Penalty in Canada, Amnesty International, n.d.
Death Penalty Database, Cornell Center on the death penalty worldwide.
Death Penalty in Middle East, International Centre of human rights, n.d.
Evans, R. J. (1996). Rituals of retribution: Capital punishment in Germany 1600–1987 (pp. 613–737 at 630 and 795).
Gracetti, G. (2014). Moving away from death penalty, 2014.
Hood, R., & Hoyle, C. (1996a). The death penalty—Worldwide perspective (p. 67).
Hood, R., & Hoyle, C. (1996b). The death penalty—Worldwide perspective (p. 115).
Hood, R., & Hoyle, C. (1996c). The death penalty—Worldwide perspective (p. 91).

Hood, R., & Hoyle, C. (1996d). The death penalty—Worldwide perspective (p. 42).
Hood, R., & Hoyle, C. (1996e). The death penalty—Worldwide perspective (p. 43).
Malone, A. (2009). China's hi-tech 'death van' where criminals are executed and then their organs are sold on black market. Mail Online.
Marazziti, M. (2014a). Moving away from death penalty, Chapter 4 (p. 170).
Marazziti, M. (2014b). Moving away from death penalty, Chapter 4 (p. 179).
Peiffer, E. (2005). The death penalty in traditional Islamic law and as interpreted in Saudi Arabia and Nigeria. *William and Mary Journal of Woman and Law, 11*(3).
Pinto, I. H. (2012). Europe: An almost death penalty-free continent, Death Penalty Worldwide, Cornell Law School, 04 May 2012.
Popoola, O. (2017). Africa must move away from death penalty.
Principe, M. L. (2000). Albert Venn Dicey and the principles of the rule of law: Is justice blind? A comparative analysis of the United States and Great Britain.
Mixed Reports on Iran Teen Hanging, Elizabeth Weill-Greenberg, n.d.
Radzinowicz, L. (1948). A history of English Criminal Law, Vol. 1, The Movement of Reform (pp. 5, 155).
Report of Human Rights Committee, General Assembly, Official Records, 53rd Session, Vol. 1, Suppl. No. 40, 1998 (p. 81).
Snyman, J. (2018). Should we bring back death penalty? 26 January 2018.
South African Institute of Race relations, 2016.
State v Makwanyane and Mchunu, 1985, CCT3/94.
The Death Penalty in Saudi Arabia: Facts and Figures, Amnesty International, 25 August 2015.
Toussiant, P. (1999). The death penalty and the "Fairy Ring" in Council of Europe, The Death Penalty: Abolition in Europe (pp. 29–34).
The Campaign for the Abolition of the Death Penalty in the African Continent, World Coalition Against Death Penalty, n.d.
World and Europe Day against the Death Penalty, European Union External Action, n.d.

Chapter 2
Death Penalty: An Indian Context

2.1 Introduction

Societies are dynamic and laws undergo modification with global reforms. In India too, laws have been modified and a few have been formulated keeping in view the crime rate and the as an influence of global reforms. Even societal views have undergone alterations and transformations with changes in technology, information, and global reforms. Significant legislative developments have expanded the role of death penalty in different legislations of the country. On December 24, 2017, a bill was passed in the state of Madhya Pradesh that introduced capital punishment in case of rape of a minor girl. An overview reveals that a number of other states have adopted similar strategies in 2017. The government of Rajasthan (Times of India, 2017) and Karnataka (Outlook, 2017) announced that they would be bringing similar legislative changes in near future.

Similarly, the year of 2017 presented significant challenges for the study of death penalty in India. There has been a drop of nearly 27% in the number of prisoners sentenced to death by Session Courts in 2017 (National Law University Delhi, 2017). The numbers, released after conducting a survey each year, have undergone a significant change. The total number of prisoners sentenced to death in 2016 now stands at 149 whereas earlier the number was 136 (National Law University Delhi, 2018). The total death row population increased from 397 to 399 by the end of 2016 (National Law University Delhi, 2017).

However, the emergence of the constitutional regulation of death penalty in India with "rarest of rare" standard has been decreed by the Court. This unique "rarest of the rare" doctrine is not absolute denunciation of life. Data indicates that there is a significant difference between death sentences pronounced and the actual executions. According to the Asian Centre for Human Rights (ACHR) report based on National Crime Records Bureau (NCRB) data, several death sentences were pronounced between 2001 and 2011, but only a few of these have actually been carried out (Hindustan Times, 2016).

S. P. Sahni and M. Junnarkar, *The Death Penalty*,
https://doi.org/10.1007/978-981-15-3129-3_2

Correspondingly, every year, Amnesty International publishes figures indicating the use of the death penalty worldwide. These figures are used as reference by the media, governments, the United Nations, and other inter-governmental bodies while analyzing the issue of capital punishment (Amnesty International, 2018).

This chapter presents a review of literature on the pre-constitutional history of the death penalty in India with different law commission reports which played a major role in the amendments. In the latter half of the chapter, the constitutionality of death penalty with landmark cases will be discussed. Lastly, the chapter will cover the laws on death penalty and method of execution in India. The chapter will conclude with the current position and ongoing changes till date.

2.2 Pre-constitutional History

In August 2015, there was a development demonstrating political opinion in favor of the abolition of death penalty in India. Similarly, an early attempt also took place in pre-independence India, when a bill for the abolition of death penalty was introduced by Gaya Prasad Singh in 1931. However, it was defeated (Law Commission of India, 35th Report, 1967). Corresponding to this, in March 1931, another proposition was made after the execution of Bhagat Singh, Sukhdev, and Rajguru by the British Government (The Hindu, 2015).

Moving on to the post-independence movements, it has been observed that from 1947 to 1949, there were questions raised on death penalty and its execution procedure. It has been observed that the nature of execution was judge-centric and there was no set rule to award death penalty in certain cases. Such orders were arbitrary in nature and it becomes important to see the factors involved in decision-making by the Hon'ble Court. Moreover, the impact of such decisions is measured by its effect on the people and the possibility of error (Constituent Assembly Debates, 3rd June 1949, Part II).

2.3 Laws and Law Commission Reports on Death Penalty in India

The relevant laws and procedures that contain the death sentence in India can be found in the Indian Penal Code (IPC) and in certain special or local legislations. The parent section, from where this power originated, is found in Section 53 of the IPC. It is the general source of authority on death sentence. The following provisions under the IPC provide for capital punishment (Table 2.1).

Besides the IPC, several laws prescribe the death penalty as a possible punishment in India. Table 2.2 indicates the Capital Offences in other Laws.

Table 2.1 Capital offences in Indian Penal Code, 1860

S. no.	Section number	Description
1.	Section 121	Treason, for waging war against the Government of India
2.	Section 132	Abetment of mutiny actually committed
3.	Section 194	Perjury resulting in the conviction and death of an innocent person
4.	Section 195A	Threatening or inducing any person to give false evidence resulting in the conviction and death of an innocent person
5.	Section 302	Murder
6.	Section 305	Abetment of a suicide by a minor, insane person or intoxicated person
7.	Section 307 (2)	Attempted murder by a serving life convict
8.	Section 364A	Kidnapping for ransom
9.	Section 376A	Rape and injury which causes death or leaves the woman in a persistent vegetative state
10.	Section 376E	Certain repeat offenders in the context of rape
11.	Section 120B	Criminal Conspiracy to commit offences
12.	Section 396	Dacoit with murder

Source Fig. 2. Law Commission of India Report (August 2015)

2.3.1 Law Commission Reports

(a) **The 35th Report of the Law Commission**

The 35th Law Commission Report of 1967 mainly discusses capital punishment and how it needs to be retained. The Commission suggested that the punishment on death penalty should be awarded at the discretion of the Hon'ble Court, with the proviso that "the vesting of such discretion or working discretion is necessary and the provisions conferring such discretion are working satisfactorily" (The 35th Law Commission Report, 1967). The report also discussed the recommendations on the issues of right to appeal in cases of death penalty to Supreme Court or High Court. It conferred on retaining of Section 303 of Indian Penal Act, 1860 which provides mandatory death penalty. However, the same was held unconstitutional by the Hon'ble Supreme Court in the case of Mithu v. State of Punjab (1983)2 SCC 277.

Table 2.2 Capital offences under other laws

S. no.	Section number	Act
1.	Sections 34, 37, and 38(1)	The Air Force Act, 1950
2.	Section 3(1)(i)	The Andhra Pradesh Control of Organized Crime Act, 2001
3.	Section 27(3)	The Arms Act, 1959 (repealed)
4.	Sections 34, 37, and 38(1)	The Army Act, 1950
5.	Sections 21, 24, 25(1)(a), and 55	The Assam Rifles Act, 2006
6.	Section 65A(2)	The Bombay Prohibition (Gujarat Amendment) Act, 2009
7.	Section 65A(2)	The Bombay Prohibition (Gujarat Amendment) Act, 2009
8.	Sections 14, 17, 18(1)(a), and 46	The Border Security Force Act, 1968
9.	Sections 17 and 49	The Coast Guard Act, 1978
10.	Section 4(1)	The Commission of Sati (Prevention) Act, 1987
11.	Section 5	The Defence of India Act, 1971
12.	Section 3	The Geneva Conventions Act, 1960
13.	Section 3 (b)	The Explosive Substances Act, 1908
14.	Sections 16, 19, 20(1)(a), and 49	The Indo-Tibetan Border Police Force Act, 1992
15.	Section 3(1)(i)	The Karnataka Control of Organized Crime Act, 2000
16.	Section 3(1)(i)	The Maharashtra Control of Organized Crime Act, 1999
17.	Section 31A(1)	The Narcotics Drugs and Psychotropic Substances Act, 1985
18.	Sections 34, 35, 36, 37, 38, 39, 43, 44, 49(2)(a), 56(2), and 59	The Navy Act, 1957
19.	Section 15(4)	The Petroleum and Minerals Pipelines (Acquisition of rights of user in land) Act, 1962
20.	Sections 16, 19, 20(1)(a), and 49	The Sashastra Seema Bal Act, 2007
21.	Section 3(2)(i)	The Scheduled Castes and Scheduled Tribes (Prevention of Atrocities) Act, 1989
22.	Section 3(1)(i)	The Suppression of Unlawful Acts against Safety of Maritime Navigation and Fixed Platforms on Continental Shelf Act, 2002
23.	Sections 10(b)(i) and 16(1)(a)	The Unlawful Activities Prevention Act

Source Fig. 3. Law Commission of India Report (August 2015)

(b) The 187th Report of the Law Commission

The 187th Report of the Law Commission came out in 2003 discussing the "Mode of Execution of Death and Incidental Matters." The report mainly confined itself around three matters: (The 187th, The Law Commission of India, 2003):

(a) The method of execution of death sentence;
(b) The process of eliminating differences in judicial opinions; and
(c) The need to provide a right of appeal to the accused by the Supreme Court in death sentence matters.

2.4 Constitutionality of Death Penalty

The Bachan Singh case of 1980 is a landmark case deciding on the issue of constitutionality of death penalty. The 1970s was a tumultuous period when the case came up before the Supreme Court. The rigidity of the law was reduced through the number of judicial modifications that came up subsequently. A traditionalist approach was taken by the Bench in Bachan Singh case to interpret the legal provisions in the light of death penalty. The majority ruling dismissed the claim that the punishment of death penalty as provided in Section 302 of IPC was unconstitutional and violated Articles 14, 19, and 21. Also, it was ruled that it would be wrong to call the subjective discretion of the judges to be arbitrary or strange.

The guidelines laid in the Bachan Singh case have to be followed and "a balance sheet of aggravating and mitigating circumstances has to be drawn up. In doing so, the mitigating circumstances have to be accorded full weightage and a just balance has to be struck between the aggravating and the mitigating circumstances before the option is exercised." The case of Bachan Singh was discussed in the light of three broad justifications for death penalty, namely, (i) reformation, (ii) retribution, and (iii) deterrence. Justice Bhagwati took the view that retribution is understood in the sense of vengeance. A huge chunk of the Indian Judgments depicts a trend to seek revenge which is quite prevalent. On the issue of deterrence, it becomes difficult to establish a relation between death penalty and its ability to deter prospective criminals.

2.5 Some of the Factors That Affect Sentencing and the Review of Sentencing

The Supreme Court has held that awarding death sentence should only be in the rarest of the rare case as in the case of (Bachan Singh v. State of Punjab, 1980). In order to ensure that the death penalty is not imposed routinely and in a mechanical manner, the court has evolved a mechanism to arrive at a conclusion, i.e., whether or not a particular case falls within the rarest of the rare case criteria. No uniform principle can be laid down for categorizing the instances of crime as a rarest of the rare case. Crime is the result of several causes and hence each case has to be decided in the context and merits in which the crime is committed. Some crimes are committed at the spur of the moment, without premeditation or planning, sometimes to save one's life or even other's life. In these circumstances, the court cannot lose sight of these factors which played a crucial role in crime causation. The Supreme Court considers this as a mitigating factor, and refrains from awarding death penalty, in order to balance the equities. Therefore, in imposition of death penalty, there is no uniform standard followed by the Supreme Court. This can be studied by analyzing the sentencing pattern in various kinds of cases.

2.6 Gender-Based Violence

Among the cases which are contentious from the point of view of the death sentence are the gender-based violence crimes. The prominent cases which come before the court are dowry murders, rape cases, and also rape and murder. The heinousness of the crime and public sentiments make these cases sensational; however, often indecisive approach is opted. Some of the gender-based violence parameters and legal scenarios are discussed below.

2.7 Dowry Murder

The issue of dowry-based violence became the center of attention with the rise of the women's movement in 1980s. The Supreme Court has emphasized the evils of dowry in the society. In reality, it has never had a chance to uphold the capital punishment in the dowry murder case. The case of the State (Delhi Administration) v. Laxman Kumar and others, 1986 was one of the first cases on "dowry death" which brought forward the atrocities of the crime. The trial sentenced the three accused with death penalty which was thereafter overturned by the High Court. This was deeply criticized as the High Court as the court failed to provide cogent reasons and pushed the issue under the carpet. In fact, the High court went on ranting about the ills of "dowry death" and reasoned that a sentence as of the trial court is likely to trigger public sentiments, especially women's organizations. In the case of Virbhan Singh and Anr versus State of U.P., 1983, the court took a positive approach stating that the facts make a heinous case for dowry death and the accused is guilty beyond reasonable doubt. The Court, acting as the guardian, took upon itself the duty to award the maximum punishment prescribed by the law for such offences. This would not only serve as a deterrent to the prospective criminals but also highlight the sensitivity of such anti-social crimes. However, this case pointed out that the Supreme Court is not much affected by the public wrath. Similarly, in another case of Attorney General of India versus Lachma Devi and others, 1986, the High court was mocked for taking the emotion head-on. Licchamadevi versus State of Rajasthan, 1988, case devised an ideology which has long been followed by the courts in India since then. The judge's discretion to award death sentence should hatch on strong reasons instead of public emotion and wrath. The Supreme Court, in its analysis, has pointed out the evils of dowry but it never had the chance to uphold a death sentence in case of dowry murder.

2.8 Rape and Murder Cases

The Supreme Court has, through its various judgments, failed to uphold death sentence in case of rape and murder of adult woman. However, when the victim was a minor, the Court showed no such hesitation to impose death sentence. This attitude, though shocking, is clear from the following judgments of the Supreme Court. In Prakash Mahadeo Godse v. State of Maharashtra, 1969, in which the Supreme Court had overturned the lower court's decision to award death penalty and the accused were acquitted on several grounds, including factual inconsistency. In other cases, including State of Maharashtra v. Manglya Dhavu Kongil, 1972, where the Supreme Court overturned the lower court's sentence of acquittal, it did not go to the extent of awarding death penalty. This act of the Supreme Court was nothing short of fence-sitting. Despite warnings by the High Court that sparing the accused would be setting a sex maniac free in the society, the Supreme Court did not award death penalty. The idea behind the High Court's reasoning could be to introduce the element of deterrence in the society. This approach of the court in not awarding death sentence is reprehensible.

2.9 Rape and Murder of Minors

Under this category, the approach of the Court is in remarkable contrast with the preceding category. While in the previous category, the court had expressed reservations in awarding death sentence; in this category, the Court has, over a period of time, been more receptive and inclined to award capital punishment. However, despite this sentiment, many accused were acquitted. The period between 1990 and 1999 saw progression, with the Supreme Court upholding the death sentence. In the case of Mohan Anna Chavan v. State of Maharashtra, 2008, the offence of raping and murdering two minor girls under the age of ten was called "beastly" that qualified under the rarest of the rare category. Deterrence was the prime reason given by the Supreme Court for awarding the death penalty.

In Dhananjoy Chatterjee alias Dhana v. State of West Bengal, 1994, a security guard was sentenced for raping and murdering a minor girl who was a resident of the same building. The security guard, who is required to assume the role of a protector, became her predator due to his lascivious acts. The Court emphasized the aggravating factors, such as the acquaintance of the accused with the victim and breach of faith by the security guard. Three days after the execution of Dhanonjoy Chatterjee which took as long as 13 years, another similar case came up, Rahul alias Raosaheb v. State of Maharashtra, 2005. The irony is that in the former case, the accused was executed for being a peril to the society but in the latter case, the accused was let off with life imprisonment. Huge disparities came about. They were reasoned by the court as: "*Some criminals get very harsh sentences while many receive grossly different sentence for an essentially equivalent crime and a shockingly large number even go unpunished thereby weakening the system's credibility.*" A diametrically opposite stance taken by the Supreme Court within a span of 3 days, rewords the absurdity and paradoxical nature of the Judges' stance on death penalty in India.

Another striking case, Laxman Naik v. State of Orissa, 1995, shows that the Supreme Court does not consider it proper to award punishment other than death if it involves rape and murder of a child. Here the Court remarked, "*the act of rape and murder of a minor girl by her paternal uncle sends shocking waves not only to the judicial conscience but to everyone having slightest sense of human values and particularly to the blood relations and the society at large.*" In another similar case of Magani Rajani Jyoti v State of Odisha, 2003, where a person took away his niece under the pretext of providing future job prospects and raped her. This act was also grievous enough to impose death penalty. However, the accused got away with a scanty punishment of 7-year imprisonment. Familial bond, which is considered sacrosanct, had been tainted. Such cases attract social censure for abusing the issue of trust of the family members. The effect of circumstantial evidence on the imposition of death penalty has been considered by the Supreme Court in the case of Kamta Tiwari v state of Madhya Pradesh, 1996. In this case, death was not the result of the rape but it was suspected that it was a case of murder with rape. The Court reasoned as follows: "*The crime was not premeditated or intentional and the death could have been due to gagging while the act of rape was being committed. The dubiousness of the cause of death forms the circumstantial evidence. The death was not overtly committed and in fact was a consequence of the act of the accused. The offence could look brutal but fails to qualify as the rarest of the rare case.*" In another case, Rameshbhai Chandubhai Rathod v. State of Gujarat, 2011, the court noted the young age of the accused. On the basis of the perpetrator's age, the court felt that the perpetrator stood a strong chance of reformation, and hence the Court did not pronounce the death sentence.

In the case of State of U.P. v. Satish, 2005, the court changed its three-decade-long attitude and came up with an out-of-the-box reasoning. The case became a recent exception when the Supreme Court took a conscious step of actively awarding death penalty. The instant case was categorized under the head of "rarest of the rare," and the accused was given a death sentence. However, such approach was criticized as throwing caution to the winds by ignoring the three-decade-old judicial prudence and was called unwarranted and unwise.

2.10 Infidelity and Jealousy

Most of the cases involving infidelity and sexual jealousy form a small part of the judgments involving gender violence. In such cases, the court has been unwilling to uphold death sentences. This disinclination has been evident by giving sexual jealousy as a mitigating factor. In another case, (Moorthy v. State of Tamil Nadu, 1988), "disappointment of a discarded lover" was considered as a mitigating factor to do away with the death sentence. The Court further observed in this case that the aggravation in accused's mental condition was fuelled by viewing a violent film a night before the murder and therefore "*society cannot be completely absolved from sharing the responsibility of the resulting tragedy.*" However, certain exceptions are attracted too. The Supreme Court gave reasons that the crime was "*most heinous, cold-blooded and gruesome murder" that "sends a chill down our spine and shocks our judicial conscience.*" In the case of Bheru Singh s/o Kalyan Singh vs. State of Maharashtra, 1994, where despite discernible repentance of the accused, the capital punishment was not awarded. In this case, a man murdered his wife along with children; however, the infidelity of his wife was questioned. In spite of this, the Court went ahead to award the death sentence. The irrationality in the death sentence seems evident through the judgments delivered.

Thus, from the above case discussions, it can be concluded that in dowry cases and rape cases, the Supreme Court has rather been reluctant to award death penalty. While in cases concerning rape and murder, the Supreme Court has shown remarkable zeal in not tolerating such abhorrent acts and dealt with them with an iron hand by imposing death penalty in most of the cases. This anomaly in awarding the death sentence adversely affects the precedents that would develop subjectivity in the imposition of death penalty.

2.11 Age as a Criterion in Sentencing

Prior to the case of Bachan Singh, the Supreme Court was clueless on how to deal with the cases involving youth and juveniles. Although the issue of age was acknowledged, it failed to become a substantial reason for the Supreme Court to commute the death sentence. In Jay Kumar v. State of Madhya Pradesh, 1999, the Supreme Court refused to commute the sentence awarded to the appellant, a young man aged 22 years, who murdered his sister-in-law in a failed attempt to rape her. Thereafter, the accused hanged her mauled head from a tree. In addition, he also killed her 8-year-old daughter for being the sole witness. However, in the case of (Balraj v. State of U.P, 1995), the Court commuted the sentence of the appellant who chopped off a man's head and threw it at his door front after parading it through the village. This case is a plausible example of the rarest of the rare doctrine; however, the accused was awarded life imprisonment in light of some mitigating circumstances. In another case of Amit alias Ammu v. State of Maharashtra, 2003, the age bar was further reduced to 20 years of age for the accused who took a school girl of the age of 12 to an isolated place and strangulated her to death after raping her. The high court was of the view that the instant case falls under the category of “rarest of the rare” criterion. The Supreme Court on appeal confirmed the sentence. However, in view of various reasons like no previous record of crime, the young age of the accused, no evidence of him being a danger to society, the sentence was reduced to life imprisonment. Different stances taken by the Supreme Court in various cases raise questions and doubts on the whimsicality in upholding or commuting the death sentence.

2.12 Juvenile Offenders

The very concept that death sentence should not be given to juveniles got acknowledged for the first time in 1967 in the 35th Law Commission Report on Capital Punishment. This position was stated again in the 42nd report on reform of the Indian Penal Code in 1971. As a part of this, an amendment was drafted. The Bill could not have been passed; however, it was a part of India’s obligation of the International Human Rights, thus demanding India to take legal steps in international direction. In some cases, minor age of an offender was considered a mitigating factor as it is a tender age and the aim of the judgement should be reformative in nature. This is because it is assumed that the minors would not know the consequences of their actions at this age. In many cases, no evidence was found to ascertain the actual age of the offender as provided by the prosecution.

2.13 Reformation and Restoration of the Offender

This factor hinges on the idea of providing “special reasons” for giving capital punishment as mentioned in the Section 354(3) of the new Criminal Penal Code in the year 1973. The underlying theme is the reformation of the offender and restoring him back to the society. This is far from the idea of retribution and deterrence. In Sections 360 and 361 of the criminal Penal Code, the court also used “special reasons” to give benefit of doubt if conditions were “such as to compel the Court to hold that it is impossible to reform and rehabilitate the offender after examining the matter with due regard to the age, character and antecedents of the offender and the circumstances in which the offence was committed.” The above changes were consolidated in the new CrPC 1973 and are reflective of the fact that the legislature has been very receptive of the emerging trends of criminology. Also, it was indeed the Bachan Singh’s case which brought forward the idea of “rarest of the rare” cases.

2.14 Mental Health

Death penalty to mentally deranged people has been viewed by the courts in different ways. Though mental illness is a general exception under the criminal law, the court has considered various other factors in adjudicating the sentencing, particularly in imposing death sentence. To pledge mental illness as a reason to commute death sentence to life imprisonment was accepted as early as in 1961 by the trial and high courts. In one case—Gopalan Nair versus The State of Kerala, 1973—the accused, due to prior mental illness, was admitted to a mental hospital. The trial court refused to accept the defence of unsoundness of mind even after the clear failure of prosecution to put before the court an alternative motive. However, the apex court commuted death sentence, since there was "nothing to show that he was not suffering from a mental obsession which may not amount to insanity but which may affect a person's mind in a way quite different from that of a normal person." The world community recognizes the principle of sparing insane people from execution. The accused have to be declared mentally ill at the time of crime or even execution. The reason behind this is the incapacity of such people to understand what the consequences of their crimes would entail and also because of impairment of judgment and inability to be aware of their actions or of the punishments that would be inflicted on committing such an offence.

2.15 Other Factors

Socioeconomic background of the offenders and even their caste and religion have been given very little attention while adjudicating the sentence to be awarded by the courts. The courts have refused to consider religion and other subliminal factors in the judicial process while awarding death penalty. Hence, it is difficult to assume the interference of any such factors which assist the court in sentencing.

2.16 Caste

Caste is a dominant factor in India. It plays a huge role in social, religious, and regional spheres, with varying degrees. However, very little discussion and deliberation related to this factor take place when it comes to death penalty sentencing. This may be attributed to very little evidence suggesting caste being a factor in factual matrix leading to the crime. Usually, in case of mass caste-based killings, the caste factor is at the forefront.

2.17 Religion

Crimes committed in the context of religion or resulting from communal clashes have led to a death sentence to a very small extent and such cases have seldom reached the Supreme Court. In the case of Dharma Rama Bhagare v. The State of Maharashtra, 1973, the court came to the conclusion that it is "not only destructive of our basic traditional social order founded on toleration in recognition of the dignity of the individual and of other cherished human values, but also has a tendency to mar our national solidarity." But this attitude saw a sea change after 1984 anti-Sikh riots that took place as an aftermath of Indira Gandhi's assassination. The courts considered that the killing would be a mitigating factor rather than the aggravating factor.

In Lokeman Shah v. State of West Bengal, 2001, an unlawful assembly was set up to avenge the defilement of mosque by a person. The accused was also a part of the unlawful assembly which caused the death of the person. However, the death sentence was reduced to life imprisonment. The court's reasoning flourished on the ground that the killing was unguided by reason and effectuated by a delirious psyche.

2.18 Politics

The Supreme Court has leaned toward a lenient view in cases of crimes committed in the political setting. In the case of Apren Joseph alias Current Kunjukunju and ors. v. the State of Kerala, 1973, the court reduced death sentence to life imprisonment on the argument that "excessive zeal for their party felt unduly provoked by the success of the meeting organized by the Karshak Sangham and being misguided by political intolerance and cult of violence they committed the offences in question soon after the said meeting." The court viewed that the offenders were motivated by political zest and considered it as a mitigating factor. However, the court clarified that they were not laying down any ground rules with regard to political murders.

In awarding the death penalty, courts have always trod cautiously and endeavored to award death penalty only in extreme cases. This could be seen from their attitude, especially in cases of rape and murder of a minor. It is also noteworthy, after a complete factual analysis of the cases that mitigating circumstances have been a major ground to taper off the punishment. This could be inferred from the adjudication of penalty in infidelity cases, communal violence, and even political offences.

References

Articles:

Death penalty: 'Rarest of rare' cases are not so rare in India now. *Hindustan Times*, February 05, 2016.

Rajasthan Government contemplates death penalty for minors. *Times of India*, December 14, 2017.

After Madhya Pradesh, Karnataka plans a law to give death penalty to rapists for minor girls. *Outlook*, December 24, 2017.

Special Correspondent, It's time death penalty is abolished: Aiyar. *The Hindu*, 7 August, 2015. Retrieved May 21, 2018, from https://www.thehindu.com/news/national/its-time-death-penalty-is-abolished-aiyar/article7509444.ece.

Reports:

Amnesty International. (2018). *Death penalty*. Data Source https://www.amnesty.org/en/what-we-do/death-penalty/

The Death Penalty in India: Annual Statistics 2016, Centre on Death Penalty, National Law University Delhi, February 2017.

The Death Penalty in India: Annual Statistics 2017, Centre on Death Penalty, National Law University Delhi, January 2018.

Law Commission of India, 35th Report 1967, at para 12. Retrieved May 21, 2018, from https://lawcommissionofindia.nic.in/reports/report262.pdf.

Law Commission of India, 187th Report 2003. Retrieved May 21, 2018, from https://lawcommissionofindia.nic.in/reports/187th%20report.pdf.

Constituent Assembly Debates, 3rd June 1949, Part II. Retrieved May 21, 2018, from https://indiankanoon.org/doc/348883/.

Law Commission of India Report No.262, The Death Penalty August 2015. Retrieved May 21, 2018, from https://lawcommissionofindia.nic.in/reports/report262.pdf.

Statues:

Criminal Law Amendment Ordinance, 2018, Ministry of Law and Justice, Page 1.

Cases:

Bachan Singh v. State of Punjab AIR 1980 SC 898 (Ind.)

State (Delhi Administration) v. Laxman Kumar and ors AIR 1986 SC 250 (Ind.)

Virbhan Singh AndAnr versus State OfU.P 1983 SCR (3) 600 (Ind.)

Attorney General of India v. Lachma Devi and others AIR 1986 SC 467 (Ind.)

Licchamadevi v. State of Rajasthan AIR 1988 SC 1785 (Ind.)

Prakash MahadeoGodse v. State of Maharashtra 1969 3 SCC 741 (Ind.)

State of Maharashtra v. ManglyaDhavuKongil AIR 1972 SC 1797 (Ind.)

Mohan Anna Chavan v. State of Maharashtra 2008 7 SCC 561 (Ind.)
Dhananjoy Chatterjee alias Dhana v. State of West Bengal 1994 2 SCC 220 (Ind.)
Rahul alias Raosaheb v. State of Maharashtra 2005 10 SCC 322 (Ind.)
LaxmanNaik v. State of Orissa AIR 1995 SC 1387 (Ind.)
MaganiRajaniJyoti v State of Odisha 2003 CrLJ 530 (ori) (Ind.)
Kamta Tiwari v. State of Madhya Pradesh AIR 1996 SC 2800 (Ind.)
RameshbhaiChandubhaiRathod v. State of Gujarat 2011 2 SCC 764 (Ind.)
State of U.P. v. Satish AIR 2005 SC 1000 (Ind.)
Moorthy v. State of Tamil Nadu 1988 3 SCC 207 (Ind.)
Bheru Singh s/o Kalyan Singh v. State of Maharashtra 1994 2 SCC 467 (Ind.)
Jay Kumar v. State of Madhya Pradesh AIR 2004 SC 3508 (Ind.)
Balraj v. State of U.P AIR 1995 SC 1935 (Ind.)
Amit alias Ammu v. State of Maharashtra AIR 2003 SC 3131 (Ind.)
Gopalan Nair v. The State of Kerala 1973 1 SCC 469 (Ind.)
Dharma Rama Bhagare v. The State of Maharashtra 1973 1 SCC 537 (Ind.)
Lokeman Shah v State of West Bengal 2001 CrLJ 2353 (Ind.)
Apren Joseph alias Current Kunjukunju and ors. v. the State of Kerala AIR 1973 SC 1 (Ind.)

Chapter 3
Role of Non-state Actors in Death Penalty

Non-state actor has the most volatile definition. Studies tend to define non-state actors depending on the substrata these want to focus. Since it is not a homogeneous category, domestic and international laws use the term befitting their own set of standards. Failure to come to terms with a common standard definition for such an amorphous term does not neglect the relevance a non-state actor holds in influencing the fate of Death Penalty nationally as well as transnationally. The role and influence of non-state actors have witnessed an upward swing in the backdrop of globalization and privatization.

3.1 Introduction

For understanding what a non-state is, understanding what a state is, becomes the priority of the chapter. State popularly understood in the public international law is the one having a permanent population, a defined territory, government, and capacity to enter into relations with other states. However, Article 1 of Montevideo Convention on the Rights and Duties of States of 1993 states all these requirements to be essential but not exhaustive. It means any individual or organization allied to any particular state becomes a state actor. Whereas any individual or organization that has significant political influence but not allied to any state becomes a non-state actor. Non-state actor is thus referred to (but not limited to) the diverse range of entities from civil societies to armed and paramilitary forces, from NGOs to drug cartels, from universities and research institutes to multinational corporations, from media to trade unions, from religious groups to criminal organizations. Such a wide spectrum and just one term!

As per Article 6 of the Cotonou Agreement, non-state actors include.

- The private sector;
- Economic and social partners, including trade union organizations; and.
- Civil society in all its diversity, according to national characteristics (ACP Group, 2003).

S. P. Sahni and M. Junnarkar, *The Death Penalty*,
https://doi.org/10.1007/978-981-15-3129-3_3

The term non-state actor, thus, may refer to a wide spectrum of developmental actors that are not allied to governments or their institutions. Though the definition is broad, it clearly recognizes the diversity when it mentions "civil society in all its forms".

To be "eligible", non-state actors must.

- Address the needs of the population;
- Have specific competencies;
- Be organized and lead democratically and transparently (ACP Group, 2003).

Subsequently, a non-state actor can be defined as a self-motivating and self-resourcing entity having a free choice of structure or no structure (often), undertaking "transnational" operations causing transnational impact through information access, information flows, equipment and technology access, cross-border movement and network building and "franchising". It acts as a defence to dysfunctional state. It empowers individuals and makes up for weakness of defunct states.

3.2 Death Penalty and Non-State Actors

Capital Punishment has been a matter of academic and non-academic debates (abolitionist vs. retentionist) and discussions for eons. It is based on the philosophy of "just deserts" (=justly deserved), a philosophy of justice. From the perspective of criminal justice system, death penalty is instituted in many countries in the form of deterrence or in the form of retribution. On various occasions, the state as well as non-state actors have questioned the relevance of death penalty and demanded prohibition. Those in favor of death penalty do not regard rehabilitation and are purely based on the black letter of law. The motivation is the apparent deterrent effect which it has on society, and even though empirically, if this statement cannot be said to be true, one of the instant rebuttals is that irrespective of the deterrent effect, the state has still eradicated a perpetrator. This disregards the perpetration of monopolized violence exercised by the state.

For the convenience of readers, this chapter will deal only with those non-state actors who have a direct or indirect influence in influencing the policy-making of Death Penalty. The non-state actors dealt further in the chapter are mentioned below:

(3.2.1) United Nations Human Rights Office of the High Commissioner,
(3.2.2) Amnesty International,
(3.2.3) International Commission Against Death Penalty,
(3.2.4) World Coalition Against Death Penalty,
(3.2.5) Sant'Egidio,
(3.2.6) Ensemble Contre la Peine de Mort,
(3.2.7) Amicus,
(3.2.8) Criminologists, and
(3.2.9) Media.

3.2.1 United Nations Human Rights Office of the High Commissioner and Death Penalty

Non-state actors are prime movers in today's world, and the United Nations (UN) needs to be more pro-active in "bringing together all constituencies relevant to global issues and galvanizing appropriate networks for effective results", says the report of an independent panel chaired by former Brazilian President Fernando Henrique Cardoso (UN, 2004). UN is a global voice for non-state actors since it opposes the use of capital punishment in all circumstances. It becomes more relevant in those countries that retain the death penalty. They work by calling global moratorium as a step toward complete abolition. Worldwide, about 70% of the countries have abolished the capital punishment now.

International human rights law requires that those sentenced to death have the right to seek amnesty, pardon or commutation of the sentences. The Office of the High Commissioner for Human Rights, with its mandate to promote and protect all human rights, advocates for the universal abolition of the death penalty. The UN Human Rights Office argues this position for other reasons as well, including the fundamental nature of the right to life; the unacceptable risk of executing innocent people; and the absence of proof that the death penalty serves as a deterrent to crime (OHCHR, n.d.).

The United Nations Human Rights office also encourages member countries, civil society, and other vital stakeholders to completely eliminate death penalty by putting an embargo in a phased manner.

In 2007, when the death penalty moratorium resolution was first adopted by the United Nations General Assembly (UN Doc. A/C.3/67/L.44/Rev.1), it was supported by 104 states. In the most recent vote in 2012, it was supported by 110 states (UNRIC, 2012). United Nations puts out its report card every 5 years on death penalty. In 1970s, around 120 countries used death penalty as a legal punishment. The number has now reduced to less than 60 in 2009 report.

The international development toward abolition can be traced through the following advancements:

1. An overwhelming majority of the world used death penalty as a legal punishment in 1960s. However, International Covenant on Civil and Political Rights (ICCPR) was actively pursuing for its abolition internationally.
2. Article 6 of the ICCPR did not bar capital punishment in all cases but also cautioned "nothing in this article shall be invoked to delay or to prevent the abolition of capital punishment by any State Party to the present Covenant." (OHCHR, n.d.)
3. In 1984, the UN Economic and Social Council adopted safeguards guaranteeing protection of the rights of those facing death penalty (OHCHR, n.d.).
4. In 1989, 33 years after the adoption of the covenant itself, the UN General Assembly adopted the Second Optional Protocol to the ICCPR that gave abolition a new decisive momentum. Member states which became parties to the protocol agreed not to execute anyone within their jurisdictions (OHCHR, n.d.).

5. In a series of four resolutions adopted in 2007, 2008, 2010, 2012, and 2013, the General Assembly urged states to respect international standards that protect the rights of those facing the death penalty, to progressively restrict its use and reduce the number of offences which are punishable by death (OHCHR, n.d.).

"The continuing application of the death penalty is a *cruel practice* that undermines human dignity," United Nations Secretary-General Ban Ki-moon said as he urged member states to "reaffirm faith in fundamental human rights" and impose moratoriums on executions. The Secretary-General noted that an increasing number of states from all regions of the world had acknowledged the failure of capital punishment as a means to exact justice. "*The taking of life is too irreversible for one human being to inflict it on another*," he continued. "*We must continue to argue strongly that the death penalty is unjust and incompatible with fundamental human rights.*"

The Office of the High Commissioner for Human Rights (OHCHR) also released a report in Geneva, entitled *Moving Away from the Death Penalty: Arguments, Trends, and Perspectives,* that accentuates the need for political leadership to take concrete steps for abolishing death penalty. "*The death penalty has no place in the twenty-first century. Leaders across the globe must boldly step forward in favour of abolition*". UN Secretary-General Ban Ki-moon's remark reflects the global trend away from capital punishment (OHCHR, 2014).

Twelve member countries of the United Nations on the occasion also made an appeal to "*jointly call for a world which respects human dignity.*" A landmark declaration was also made. In a first, foreign ministers of both abolitionist and non-abolitionist states, whilst accentuating that they respect the opinions of those member states in favor of the death penalty, declared that they "*consider that state executions should not be taking place in the twenty-first century. Modern justice systems must aspire to more than retribution.*"

Assistant Secretary-General for Human Rights, Ivan Šimonović, also celebrated the overall trend toward abolition, adding that support for abolition resonated across regions, legal systems, traditions, customs and religious backgrounds. Šimonović underscored three vital aspects in the report that aptly emphasized the need to get rid of the capital punishment, such as the need to avoid executing those subjected to wrongful convictions; the lack of statistical evidence pointing to the death penalty as a useful deterrent; and the higher rate of execution among those from marginalized communities, including people with mental or intellectual disabilities. He further added that whilst some people believed death penalty serves justice through retribution, the victims and their families "*do not want revenge but prefer justice without revenge or retribution.*"

The UN High Commissioner for Human Rights, Zeid Ra'ad Al Hussein expressed concern at deeply worrying reports during 2016 that people in Indonesia are getting death penalties for even drug-related cases. Fourteen people face death penalties in the country, most of them for drug-related offences. Al Hussein appealed to authorities to immediately reinstate a moratorium on the death penalty. His office also expressed deep concern about the complicities and lack of transparency during the course of trials. There were also concerns about the denial of the right to appeal.

Under International Covenant on Civil and Political Rights, which many countries including Indonesia has signed, it is recommended to use death penalty only in cases where the crimes are of extreme severity. The High Commissioner stressed the need to respect such international guidelines. Drug-related offences do not fall under the threshold of "most serious crimes". Even then, the case has to meet stringent fair trial standards, including full transparency throughout the process (OCHCR, n.d.). "The death penalty is not an effective deterrent relative to other forms of punishment nor does it protect people from drug abuse. The focus of drug-related crime prevention should involve strengthening the justice system and making it more effective," he said. The chief urged the Indonesian government to work on alternative strategies to combat such crimes.

In the book *Death Penalty and the Victims*, released by OCHR in 2016, the victimological aspect of death sentence receiver is explored. It presents a picture of the convict and the third parties as victims. It raises issues of mistaken execution as well as chances of discrimination arising from this kind of punishment. Moreover, it highlights how death penalty goes against ethos of international law (OCHR, 2016).

3.2.2 Amnesty International and Death Penalty

Amnesty International is a highly democratic, transparent, transnational and grassroot human rights organization of more than seven million people who take injustice personally. It is a global movement for a world free of capital punishment. As a forerunning non-state actor, it opposes the death penalty in all cases without exception, regardless of the nature or circumstances of the crime; guilt, innocence, or other characteristics of the individual; or the method used by the state to carry out the execution. The death penalty violates the right to life as proclaimed in the Universal Declaration of Human Rights. It is the ultimate cruel, inhuman, and degrading punishment (Amnesty International, 2018).

It investigates and exposes the facts, whenever and wherever abuses happen. It lobbies governments and other powerful groups such as companies making sure they keep their promises and respect international law. Since 1961, they have been helping people claim their rights across the world. They publish a report annually, reporting figures and analyzing trends for each country. Amnesty's latest report, Death Sentences and Executions 2017, was released in April 2018 (Amnesty International, 2018).

Amnesty International has been an important instrument in bringing the issue of death penalty from penumbral to umbral sphere in world affairs. It has shifted from a large London base and made regional visibility in cities of Africa, Asia-Pacific, Central and Eastern Europe, Latin America, and the Middle East. The regional offices help in catering swift and global responses to regional events in more than 70 countries.

It works by successful adoption of resolutions on a moratorium on the use of the death penalty by the UN General Assembly and applies pressure with regard to the cases that face imminent execution. They also support actions and work by the abolitionist movement at national, regional, and global levels (Amnesty International).

Amnesty International has evolved itself from categorical abolition to unqualified abolition since 1974. It was the time when abolitionist countries stood at just sixteen (Karn, 2010, p. 116). With the increasing international visibility post-winning Nobel prize for peace in 1977, AI organized Stockholm Conference of 1977 where more than 200 delegates and participants from 50 nations of the world took part. The declaration includes "total and unconditional opposition" to death penalty and recalls that the death penalty is the ultimate cruel, inhuman, and degrading punishment that violates the right to life.

The challenge in front of Amnesty International was to convince the Eastern segment of the world that abolition on Death Penalty is not another agenda to create cultural imperialism. Thomas Hammarberg, the chairman of Amnesty's International Executive Committee, highlighted how the new report (the Death Penalty report 1979) broadened the context in which abolition was considered and how it addressed the legal systems in Africa, Asia, and Latin America, as well as those in North America and Europe. It was stressed time and again that despite background, political, cultural, and social differences, the countries can stand united in their opposition to death penalty. AI has lobbied national governments and has influenced public opinion instead of waiting for public to catch up. They have got favorable views with respect to a blanket ban on death penalty de jure as well as de facto (Karn, 2010).

Amnesty initially struggled to bridge the gap between aspirations and practice. The inability to get strong UN support for death penalty abolition brought the shift in its working from idealism to pragmatism, from appeals and principles to strategic goals and tactics. Whereas twenty-six countries had abolished the death penalty by the end of 1976, the count reached eighty by the end of 1988 (Karn, 2010, p. 123). AI has raised their voice by projecting the capital punishment as a core human rights issue.

The diplomatic hobnobbing has not garnered much support of UN's groupings. Keeping that in mind, it works to develop a multipronged initiative to ensure that organizational resources would be deployed along a broad front. From being an underground movement looking for inroads to mainstream, it presents itself as a critical test case, unfolding at the center of a burgeoning human rights movement, which had been gaining strength since the end of World War II. The overall tone of AI's work has changed from apologetic and pleading to uncompromising and self-assured, with an emphasis not only on the urgency of the vision, but also on the practicality of the plan (Karn, 2010, p. 125). It emphasizes the utility of enlisting support from celebrities and public figures which has cultivated a youthful support base and also dampened the effect of public opinion polls which were pro-retentionist.

AI has been firm in its opposition to the practice of extradition of detainees and asylum seekers to countries where they might face the Death Penalty. AI has been smart in using a campaign to launch a research project to assess the extent to which the

Death Penalty had served as a barrier to extradition in Western Europe. The campaign launched was set to coincide with publication of the new Death Penalty report in April 1989 and AI pressed the national sections to add more publicity to its cause (Karn, 2010). The death penalty report "When the State kills" targeted the retentionist states as well as its citizens, projecting them responsible for executions. The report of 1989 challenged its readers to confront their government and challenge those who take away their universal rights. It reiterated that the experience of abolitionist countries gave ample evidence that the death penalty is neither desirable nor necessary.

AI has started taking more confrontational stance since its origin. At inception, when the declaration was made, very few countries had abolished death penalty. These included eight countries in Europe and eight in Americas. By the end of 1990s, another 27 countries abolished the Death Penalty either in law or in practice (though cold war leading fragmentation had a role to play, but AI's role is well-established).

In 2016, very few countries—precisely 23—carried out executions. An overwhelming majority of these executions were carried out in Asian countries like Iran, Pakistan, China, Saudi Arabia and Iraq. Today, that number has risen to 106—more than half the world's countries. In 2017, Declaration of Stockholm—the first international manifesto calling for abolition of death penalty completed its 40 years. The landmark declaration in 1977 had called on all the governments in the world to abolish the death penalty.

> When the state uses its power to end the life of a human being, it is likely that no other right is inviolate. The state cannot give life, it should not presume to take it away.

By telling the powerful stories of the people it works with, it mobilizes millions of supporters around the world to campaign for change and to stand in defence of activists on the frontline. The case study of Hafez Ibrahim, from Yemen, is one of the powerful examples talking of results that Amnesty's campaign bears. The execution was stopped not once, but twice. In 2005, it was AI that called on Yemeni President to stop his execution. Later in 2007, he sent a mobile text again stating that he is about to be executed. This led to a humongous campaign at an international level, ultimately saving him from execution. The President had to stop his execution for the second time. Hafiz now works as a lawyer who fights cases of juveniles on death penalty, across the country.

Another story is of the activist Souleymane Sow of France. Sow was an activist since his student days. He was adamant on bringing change and making a difference, so he returned to Guinea and organized a team that volunteered for Amnesty International. The aim of the group was to inculcate in people the value of a human life, essence of human rights, and need to abolish the death penalty. His team's hard work paid off as they finally succeeded in abolishing death penalty in the country. They continuously lobbied against the capital punishment every day for 5 months. In 2016, Guinea's National Assembly voted in favor of a new criminal code, which removed the death sentence from the list of applicable penalties (Amnesty International). The statistics and case studies reflect the successful picture of the non-state actor standing at the forefront and influencing the state legislations with unceasing determination.

3.2.3 *The International Commission against Death Penalty*

The International Commission against the Death Penalty (ICDP) is an outcome of an initiative launched by the Spanish Government. The mandate of the initiative was to establish a moratorium on the death penalty and to reinforce the fight against the death penalty across all regions of the world in a bid to completely do away with the abolition. The initiative at its inception was supported by 18 countries. Established on October 7, 2010 in Madrid, ICDP aims to compliment the work done by various organizations—both at international and local levels for the abolishment of the death penalty.

International Commission against Death Penalty (ICDP) acts with total independence and neutrality and works under its President Judge Navi Pillay. ICDP works with the United Nations and other international and regional organizations, governments and non-governmental organizations to further the abolition of capital punishment worldwide. The work of the ICDP is supported by a diverse group of 19 Member States and 3 Observer States from all regions of the world that are committed to abolition of the death penalty.

ICDP got recognized as a non-profit association in 2016 under Spanish law. ICDP has emerged as a very vibrant organization with its members—from different regions of the world—exerting independence in deliverance and setting up objectives. In the international arena, ICDP stands out as a premier organization working against death penalty.

In accordance with the Universal Declaration of Human Rights, ICDP holds stern opposition to the capital punishment. It is of the opinion that there is no evidence to suggest the effectiveness of deterrence theory. ICDP encourages the abolition of death penalty in those countries that observe a de facto moratorium on its use and promotes moratoriums on capital punishment in countries that rarely use it. And in countries where executions are still carried out, ICDP urges to strictly follow international rules and guidelines. ICDP also plays a pivotal role in lobbying for cases involving vulnerable groups like mentally deranged people, juveniles, and pregnant women.

To achieve these objectives, the International Commission carries out the following activities in a strategic and selective manner (ICDP):

- Collaborate and intervene before high representatives and personalities of specific countries, along with international and regional organizations and civil society representatives.
- Make appeals and statements on matters of concern relating to the abolition of the death penalty.
- Participate in conferences and seminars, as well as in campaigns to mobilize public opinion.
- Dissemination of information and presentation of papers at international forums.
- Promote intellectual and artistic works in favor of the abolition of death penalty.

From its inception, ICDP has played a pivotal role at international level in lobbying against the death penalty and encouraging legal assistance and aid to those facing capital punishment. In this regard, ICDP in 2011 participated in an international conference in Tajikistan entitled "Central Asia without the Death Penalty." Such initiatives have been continued wherein the cons of death penalty have been discussed and deliberated upon, with an aim to find ways to completely abolish it in future. ICDP has participated in conferences in Kigali, Rwanda, to find ways to encourage abolishment of capital punishment in the African continent. In a conference on the "Death Penalty in the Greater Caribbean" that was held in Madrid, it was decided to establish the first "Caribbean Network against the Death Penalty". The intention of the move was to deliberate with all the abolitionist countries in the region about measures needed to end death penalty in future.

In order to explore opportunities for working together on the issue, and to educate about the measures taken by it to promote abolition of death penalty, ICDP also met the High Commissioner of UN High Commissioner for Human Rights.

As Benin and Kyrgyzstan ratified the Second Optional Protocol to the International Covenant on Civil and Political Rights, which called for abolishing the capital punishment, ICDP welcomed the move. ICDP also welcomed Mongolia's intention to sign the protocol.

There has been a discernible trend toward abolishment of the capital punishment in the world-across all regions and different systems of law. The support at UN General Assembly for the third resolution on a moratorium on the use of the capital punishment is quite an indicator. The resolution underpins the global trend toward abolition of death penalty. Cuba released the remaining prisoners on death row, the state of Illinois in USA abolished the death penalty and South Korea passed its 5,000th day without executions in September 2011.

From the recent developments, it is clear that Africa has shown a positive trend toward the abolition of capital punishment. Very few countries in the continent are carrying out executions. At least, 36 countries have become abolitionist—in practice or law. Countries wherein the number of death penalties has increased, ICDP has either made serious interventional attempts or issued statements against the conduct of these countries.

Considering the positive developments in countries like Algeria, Morocco, and Tunisia, ICDP is specifically pushing for abolition of death penalty in these countries. In this regard, ICDP plans to hold deliberations with governments, state institutions, law-makers, and civil society members opposed to death penalty.

In Japan, death penalty is still in use. The issue is a matter of concern for ICDP. In a bid to encourage an official moratorium on the death penalty, ICDP plans to participate in a series of discussions and deliberations in the country. The Fifth World Congress against the use of capital punishment was held in Madrid in 2013. The Congress takes place every 3 years and is an attempt to bring abolitionist groups together. In certain situations, it also discusses the abolition in a—by-case manner. For example, the Arab Spring offered an opportunity to look at regional challenges, information exchange and charting out strategies for abolishment at global stage.

Recently in May this year, ICDP announced the launch of its publication, "*How States abolish the Death Penalty: 29 Case-Studies*". The report discusses the difficulties faced by 26 countries and 3 USA states as they slowly trod on the path toward complete abolition of capital punishment. This report is an improved and a more detailed version of ICDP's 2013 publication "*How States abolish the Death Penalty.*" It briefs about the interplay of various factors that are responsible for abolition such as the route of international commitment, constitutional court judgements, transitional government, constitutional amendments, role of National Assembly/Parliament, and establishment of moratorium. It has stressed the role of the international community—including the UN, the EU, and their institutions, and civil society organizations—in combination with political leadership, that played decisive role in the abolitionist process of countries like Rwanda and Spain. The organization of discussions at National Assemblies and events during the World Day against the Death Penalty was also a significant in Madagascar and Suriname (ICDP, 2018).

3.2.4 World Coalition Against Death Penalty

The idea of World Coalition Against Death Penalty came as a result of success of the first Congress. The team comprised more than thirty different organizations fighting against the death penalty during its launch in 2002 which increased to 146 in 2018 (Member Organisations). Its office is registered in France. It celebrated its first World Day Against Death Penalty in 2003, on October 10.

Since its origin, it has been unified under single thematic umbrella, i.e., abolition of the death penalty by bringing together all the abolitionist organizations. It encourages cooperation in regional coalition and formulates common strategies. The network extends to Greater Caribbean for Life (Trinidad and Tobago), Anti-Death Penalty Asia Network (Malaysia), Arab Coalition against Death Penalty (Jordan), International Academic Network for the Abolition of Capital Punishment (Spain) Parliamentarians for Global Action (USA). Every other year, it has amplified its voice toward its objective.

The year 2005 saw more than 260 separate initiatives featured in an event. The event ended with a new call to the UN to support an immediate moratorium on all executions. The publicity was extended in 2007 through five separate press conferences (in Puerto Rico, Morocco, Democratic Republic of Congo, Portugal, and the US).

Such is the aura of the initiative that it received support from several high-profile political leaders, including then Italian P.M. Romano Prodi, who pledged to put capital punishment back on the UN agenda after the details of Saddam Hussein's execution emerged in Jan 2007.

The role of this coalition has proved to be contributory among other organizations since directly or indirectly, it got success in getting its voice heard. The UNGA actually passed a resolution in December 2007 calling for a global moratorium on executions—140 voted in favor of the non-binding resolution, 54 voted against it, and 29 abstained. When UNHCR adopted the even stronger resolution in 2005, it elicited statement of dissociation from the members of the General Assembly.

The adoption of this resolution confirms and supports the global trend toward the abolition of the death penalty. Malawi and Swaziland recently also voted for the abolishment resolution for the first time. The move can be termed as a positive change toward abolishment of death penalty. Recent evolutions in abolitionist countries also lead to a positive change of vote in Malawi and Swaziland, both of which voted, for the first time, in favor of the resolution. Zimbabwe moved from opposition to abstention and Sri Lanka from abstention to a vote in favor, confirming its commitment at the time of the 6th World Congress against the Death Penalty in June 2016 (Plaçais, 2016).

Recently in 2017, WCADP stressed the socioeconomic status of prisoners during the 15th World Day against Death Penalty. The theme for 2017 was poverty. It published a methodology to motivate people to conduct a fact-finding study linking the issues at the core of the death penalty and poverty in their respective states.

In its article *Poverty and Justice—A deadly mix*, it gives an overview of studies conducted on these lines. In India, a study conducted by the National Law University of New Delhi presents interesting figures. As per the research, it was found that 74.15% of those sentenced to capital punishment (370) belong to the economically weaker sections. The number is less than that in the United States where 95% of people on death penalty belong to financially disadvantaged sections, as per a report by the Equal Justice Initiative. Similarly, in Saudi Arabia, as per the Amnesty international, though there are no numbers available, yet it is usually poor migrant workers from the Asia, Middle East, and Africa who bear the brunt of death penalty.

In Belarus, according to the Cornell Center on Death Penalty Worldwide, people with disadvantaged economic background find it difficult to bear the expenses of lawyers and other legal expenses. A study led by Amnesty International and the Legal Defence and Assistance Project (LEDAP-Nigeria) in October 2008 suggests that the overwhelming majority of the death row population in Nigeria is also comprised of economically disadvantaged people (World Coalition against the Death Penalty, 2017, p. 6).

WCADP keeps accounts of countries which have abolished death penalty in practice. It classifies further the countries on the basis of abolition or retention for all crimes, ordinary or no crimes. According to its official webpage, 23 countries carried out executions in 2017. Total 243 executions are mentioned in 2018 in which Iran tops with 36% of executions (WCADP). The top executioners being China, Iran, Saudi Arabia, Iraq, and Pakistan.

Apart from up-to-date facts and figures, it seeks response by motivating others and making them aware of what they can do to end the death penalty. It calls upon everyone—NGO's, teachers, lawyers, local representatives, member of parliaments, artists, reporters, religious leaders, and citizens alike. Some of them are writing to death row prisoners, sending support messages to next of kin of prisoners and lawyers, organizing visits to prison to understand them better and organizing public debates and discussions, public demonstrations, "sit-ins", "die-ins", "flash mobs", etc. It also organizes theater performances or short movies, screening in them families of people sentenced, exonerees, their lawyers and experts. Also it **organizes art exhibitions**.

(of artwork made by the people sentenced to death, of photographs of those on death row, of drawings or posters).

The World Coalition has developed several tools (posters, leaflets, facts and figures, detailed factsheets, and mobilization kits) and it coordinates the mobilization for 10th October all over the world to raise public awareness about the reasons as to why the people living in poverty are at a greater risk of the death penalty, and to thereby build support for abolition. It has developed a mobilization kit where it talks about the steps to organize an event like conference or symposium and how to approach people for conducting it. It is a practical worksheet which eases the procedural difficulties (World Coalition against the Death Penalty, 2017).

It calls upon governments to revisit their penal policies. It mobilizes the media to raise awareness on the issue of the death penalty. It targets **social media campaign** on Facebook and Twitter: #nodeathpenalty. It raises money through **donations** to the World Coalition Against the Death Penalty or another group working to end the death penalty.

It also contributed by participating in "Cities Against the Death Penalty/Cities for Life" on November 30, 2018, which is discussed later in the chapter. From individual to mass mobilization, it talks about the smallest act that can make a difference in the course of abolition. Their awareness outreach programs are dynamic and creative in nature and not traditional.

3.2.5 Community of Sant'Egidio and Death Penalty

Religion and its teachings have a special role in socio-cultural setting. Religion influences the common perceptions and views related to peace and non-violence in different settings. One of the religious communities is Sant'Egidio. The community was formed in 1968, after the conclusion of the second Vatican Council (under Pope Paul VI). Currently, Sant'Egidio community is present in more than 70 countries of the world and works for the marginalized people and marginalized communities across continents. The community also works for the underprivileged women and children.

Sant'Egidio Community has been working for the abolition of death penalty and helping especially those on death rows since mid-nineties. Their efforts have got recognized worldwide. According to them, "The death penalty—the extreme epitome of human rights violations, represents a means of torture, contradicts the rehabilitation perspective of justice, lowers civil society to the level of those who murder, legitimates violence at the highest level and often becomes a tool for the repression of political, ethnic or religious minorities." (Community of Sant'Egidio, n.d.).

The community reaches out to death row prisoners through correspondence followed by personal visits. It also strives through legal and other means to make prison conditions better. The first case addressed is that of Dominique Green, a young

Afro-American who was imprisoned in Texas. After Green's case, the community has reached out to more than 1500 people through a robust community network.

After 20 years of its establishment, the community launched a "Call for a Universal Moratorium" on the capital punishment. In more than 150 countries five million signatures were gathered which consisted of people of different beliefs, faiths, nationalities, and ethnicities. This was a huge step toward creating a strong front against death penalty. A day before voting for the historic resolution 62/149 of the United Nations General Assembly, the call was delivered to the Assembly which rejected the use of capital punishment as a means of serving justice (2007).

On November 21, 2014 the results of the vote in the third Committee were very encouraging. Out of 193 countries, 114 states were in favor of a "universal moratorium" on the Death penalty. Presented by 94 Member States, the moratorium also included "ringside" Italy.

The last vote in the Third Committee of November 21, 2014 gave a positive result: 114 out of 193 states represented voted in favor of the proposal for a universal moratorium presented by 94 Member States including ringside Italy.

During the vote many countries like Eritrea, Suriname, and Fiji, for the first time, subscribed to the moratorium. During a 7-year period from 2007 to 2014, votes against the proposal shot down from 52 to 36, depicting almost a 30% decline. Many countries of the Africa and Asia—which were earlier reluctant—also subscribing to the moratorium can be attributed to the prolonged extensive efforts of the Community of Sant'Egidio to make the countries aware about the human rights.

In November 2002, the first International "Cities for Life, Cities against the Death Penalty" Day was launched by the community. 30th November was chosen as a date as it coincided with the anniversary of the first death penalty abolition in the world that occurred in the "Grand Duchy of Tuscany" on November 30, 1786. In 2011, a positive outcome was observed with 78 capitals and 1936 cities from 97 countries around the world giving life to the eighth World Day "Cities for Life" through rallies, events, public performances, assemblies at educational institutes and nearby public offices.

The World Day of 'Cities for Life/Cities against the Death Penalty' is a huge and probably the largest mobilization movement for the abolition of the capital punishment in the world. Many cities across the world declare November 30 "Day for Life/against the death penalty" and then put the phrase "Cities for Life/Cities against the Death Penalty", next to the name of the city and its logo-a notice to that effect shall be sent to the Community of Sant'Egidio (Community of Sant'Egidio, n.d.).

Across the world, "1600 CITIES FOR LIFE" from 88 countries with 70 world capitals' illuminated a building—to submit their adherence to the "NO JUSTICE WITHOUT LIFE". They give life, by rallies, events, sit-ins, public shows and meetings in educational institutions to commemorate the 10th edition of the "World Day of the Cities for Life" (Community of Sant'Egidio, n.d.).

The Community of Sant'Egidio along with other organizations working at international level founded "World Coalition against the Death Penalty" in Rome in 2002.

To encourage international discourse on abolition of death penalty, the Sant'Egidio community has been organizing a "Mondial Conference of Ministers of Justice" each year since 2007. Both groups of countries—those in favor of or against the death penalty—actively participate in the conference looking out for viable solutions (Community of Sant'Egidio, n.d.).

Besides, Community of Sant'Egidio also organizes a yearly conference. Conference comprises senators of law, academics, jurists, Supreme Court members of both sets of countries—abolitionists as well as retentionists with special focus on countries of the African continent (Sant'Egidio, 2018). The conference develops new strategies to fulfill its vision. It gets increasing participation, including representatives of Asian and African countries, that are destined to consolidate in the coming years.

The religious non-state actors have stricken chord with various like-minded groups. They work and spread their message through appeals and prayers. Their religious preachings have made a long-lasting impact in establishing peace and humanity by building a constant dialog process.

3.2.6 Ensemble Contre la Peine de Mort

Ensemble Contre la Peine de Mort (**ECPM**) is an international alliance of francophone abolitionist organizations. It is renowned for organizing the World Congress Against Death Penalty, the world's largest abolitionist gathering. Their cause is focussed on universal abolition of death penalty under all circumstances. Some of their key features are as under:

- Proximity to prisoners sentenced to death—ECPM conducts judicial investigations into death rows in Morocco, Tunisia, and the United States. They support the victims of the death penalty, and their families.
- Advocacy with the highest authorities—ECPM is a part of the United Nation's Economic and Social Council, which enables it to advocate at the heart of the United Nations system. ECPM initiated the World Coalition Against the Death Penalty in 2002, which now has over 150 members like NGOs, bar associations, local bodies, etc., from around the world. ECPM conducts advocacy and public mobilization campaigns with crucial political decision-makers like European Union, African Commission on Human and People's Rights, governments, etc.
- Uniting Abolitionists from across the world—ECPM is the founder-organizer of the World Congresses Against the Death Penalty. These events have hosted a footfall of 1,300 people representing the world abolitionist movement. Ministers, parliamentarians, diplomats, activists, civil society organizations, researchers, and journalists come together every 3 years to help take successful steps to reach the goal of universal abolition of the death penalty.
- Education and awareness of abolition—ECPM works in schools to encourage young people to support the issue through drawing competitions, introductions

to journalism, and free class visits—with the help of specialists, individuals previously sentenced to death, or families of prisoners sentenced to death. ECPM participates in Gay Pride, the Fete da la Humanite, Cities for Life, and other such events to raise awareness among the public of the situation of minorities and vulnerable groups.

- Strengthening the capacity of local actors and taking action with them—ECPM fights against the isolation of activists wherever the death penalty is still in practice by supporting the formation of national and regional coalitions against the death penalty, as well as the creation of networks of abolitionist parliamentarians and lawyers. It promotes efficiency among the local partners by organizing training sessions.

Out of the ECPM's list of 22 arguments, below mentioned are some of their key arguments:

1. The death penalty violates right to life—Everyone has a right to life, liberty, and security of person.
2. The death penalty is cruel, inhuman and degrading—The death sentence forbids any hope, and thus could be considered torturous, owing to the fact that carrying out of this death sentence itself takes 20–30 years, where the prisoners are treated inhumanely and often times tortured.
3. The death penalty is not fair—Death penalty is retributive and perpetuates a cycle of violence.
4. The death penalty is not dissuasive and does not make the society safer—A state should uphold the value of life, and where it does not, it perpetrates violence. Out of the 20 safest countries in the world, except for Japan (9th) and Singapore (20th), all other countries are abolitionist.
5. The death penalty is a negation of an individual's ability to be rehabilitated—Death penalty discards any merit in favor of rehabilitation.
6. The death penalty does not indicate the democratic level of a country—This stance because it is an instrument mainly used by dictators to terrorize their people. Thus, abolition of the same would be a step toward being democratic.

3.2.7 Amicus

Amicus is charity which helps by providing representation to those facing death penalty in the United States. Their organization's belief is that death penalty is disproportionately imposed on the most vulnerable in the society, violating their right to due process and equal justice before the law. Thus, they aim to provide higher quality of legal aid and provide better justice to, into to, raise awareness of potential abuses of the defendant's rights. The Amicus Journal is a leading reporter on the significant issues affecting capital punishment which provides for dialog on issues concerning the death penalty and related topics.

Some of the key obstacles as recognized by the organization are as follows:

- Politicized Court System—A review found out that in the 15 states where judges were directly elected, the death sentence rejection was only 11%, whereas the 7 states where judges were appointed, the reversal rate was 26%. Judges and prosecutors both are subjected to electoral pressure to take a strong stance toward conviction of defendants.
- Innocence—There is an error rate of 9 out of 10 on death sentences according to the number of reversals since 1976. If flights had a chance of crashing once every ten of them took off, how safe would flights be considered?
- Race—The stance is that capital punishment is administered disproportionately on racial minorities.

"Over 75% of the murder victims in cases resulting in an execution were white, even though nationally only 50% of murder victims generally are white."—Death Penalty Information Center.

- Lethal Injections—Lethal injections are the primary method of execution for all the states and the federal government as well. Now, as overseas pharmaceutical companies have stopped exportation to the US, the states have resorted to using new and sometimes untested concoctions of drugs, which has resulted in botched and painful executions.
- Poverty and Quality of Legal Representation—The stance which is taken is that in a lot of cases the representation provided for the defendant lacks the inherent quality needed for defending against death penalty. The attorneys would be over-burdened, low-paid, or even devoid of necessary trial experience for capital punishment.

3.2.8 Criminologists and Death Penalty

Various criminologists have studied the case of death penalty from close quarters. Having a more sophisticated and scientific assessment on the question of the relevance of death penalty, they as intelligentsia hold greater say in the abolition or retention. The first departure from the philosophy of retaliation was seen in the work of utilitarian scientist Cesare Beccaria in eighteenth century.

The stand changed from legitimacy of Death Penalty to its removal with the advent of the Enlightenment. The attitude of *Sapere Aude*, "Dare to Know" caught much attention. Cesare Beccaria, an Italian criminologist from Classical School was one of the greatest thinkers of this age, who condemned death penalty. He challenged Death penalty in his treatise, *On Crimes and Punishment (1764)*. Beccaria emphasized more on prevention than punishment. The stress was to see punishment as a function of prevention not barbarism. Beccaria (1996) said that "the penalty of death is ineffectual because of the barbarity of the example it gives to men" (p. 58) (Beccaria, p. 58) The Beccaria's way of understanding death penalty did find support among the intelligentsia circles.

Dei dellite e delle pene, one of the greatest treatises in the democratic tradition is the testament to human freedom and social justice—as quoted by Beccaria's greatest admirer Sean L. Green, translated and printed in Austria, Spain, Sweden France, England, Germany, Austria, Spain, and Sweden. It sold a number of copies in America. The book's idea resonated with various abolitionist movements and Supreme court discussions as well as Thomas Jefferson's Bill on Proportioning Crimes and Punishment.

The book was a resounding success. It highlighted the question of Death Penalty. The law of Tuscany of 1786, became the first criminal law abolishing death penalty—after the series of debates reiterated the corrective capacity of punishment. It claimed "to see an end to the death penalty against any offender, present or future".

In his opinion, the atrocity of punishment is contrary to the humanitarian principle. It violates the proportionality principle and does not go down well from utilitarian logic. By execution or elimination, it fails in the prevention aspect. The punishments are fair only if performed for their primary purpose: to redeem the guilty and reinsert them into the welfare state. The maximum deterrent effect does not come from a terrible but passenger spectacle of death, which is the killing of a criminal but from the long and labored vision of a man without freedom, who became like a beast from service, who pays for his efforts the company that offended (Zavatta, 2017).

Beccaria, though, also held this opinion that death penalty may be used in one or two exceptions—if the accused is still a threat to the outside world whilst being imprisoned or when the capital punishment seems to be the only way of deterrence to stop others from committing this crime.

Another Italian criminologist known for biological determinism, Cesare Lombrosso from positivist school, rejected the viewpoint of Beccaria. Inspired from Darwin's theory of evolution, he postulated in his book *Criminal Man,* that criminals are atavistic. And when an "atavistic individual" commits some crime "society has the right to defend itself from this kind of delinquent". Lombroso was ambivalent about Death Penalty but generally supported it to correct the atavisitic being. For liberal and secular thinkers, science offered a counterweight to religion, commonsense and a tool to social advancement toward liberal society. He incorporated empirical evidence in his study. He criticized Beccaria for his abstract philosophy when he could have done a sample-based study (Lombroso, Gibson & Rafter, 2006).

A century after the work of Beccaria saw the past returning in the work of Raffaele Garafalo, vis-a-vis penal system and concept of the death penalty. Garafalo, another Italian criminologist from mid-nineteen century, defined the death row offenders as ones constituting a permanent psychic anomaly. Hence, the criminal is an individual ill-suited to live in the society, because his/ her morals are unacceptable to the society in which he/she lives. Garafalo supported the idea of death penalty which as per him was effective and legitimate. He believed in compelling criminals to atone for their guilt with every possible means. He put society's right above individual rights. The protection of society has to be above anything. The rationale for his supporting the death penalty lies in anthropology and in criminal psychology. As the death penalty in Italian Penal Code was recommended for abolition, Garafalo said that "the progress of anthropology destroying the utopias of correctional school, had shown that the phrase 'beast in human face' was not a popular metaphor, but a fact confirmed through scientific observation". Though every individual possesses a right to live in a society yet he cannot claim this right when his criminal conduct "undermines" the life of society (Zavatta, 2017). Crime is "*the effect of psychic anomalies, sediment habits, unhealthy environments, which must be fought with a penalty whose sole purpose is the elimination of evil, adapted to different types of offender born, instinctive and accidental. The individual utterly devoid of moral senses, that of justice and feelings of pity, will be unable to adapt to social life, and therefore must be suppressed by applying Death Penalty*" (Zavatta, 2017).

Thorsten Sellin was a penologist from the twentieth century. As a pioneer of scientific criminology, he did the first of comparative studies on the death penalty in 1950s. He was a prime mover in setting up the government agencies that collect statistics on crime. He applied the combination of qualitative and quantitative methods in an exhaustive study of capital punishment in American states. He used the microscopic details from different disciplines (history, sociology, psychology, law) to formulate a comparative analysis, observing spatial as well as temporal changes with respect to crime.

Every comparison he made led him to the inevitable conclusion that executions have no discernible effect on homicidal rates (Sellin, 1959a, 1959b, p. 34). The importance of his work lies in numerous replications with the updated data. All have confirmed his finding that capital punishment does not deter homicide. Since then, a number of comparative studies reiterated the same finding that death penalty is undesirable. Hugo Adam Bedau and Michael L. Radelet, have published the results of "sustained and systematic" research purporting to show that the use of capital punishment entails an intolerable risk of mistaken executions (Radelet & Bedau, 1998). Radelet and Akers (1996) found that most criminologists do not believe that the death penalty deters violent crime. In fact, states that have the death penalty consistently have been found to have higher rates of murder than those without it (Bedau, 1998). Also, statistical findings and case studies converge to disprove the claim that the death penalty has any deterrent value as it has been seen in the study of United States homicide and execution data from 1925 to1949 (Schuessler, 1952).

Professor Edwin H. Sutherland, a pioneer of Differential Association Theory, stressed for a scientific study on death penalty offenders over a commonsensical approach or belief system to come to any conclusion establishing the direct relation between death penalty and reducing rate of homicide. In the book, Murder and the Death Penalty, it is mentioned that the States that have abolished Capital Punishment have low rates of homicides. But whether a relationship exists or not has not been proved. So far it has been a matter of commonsense (Sutherland, 1925). He says, "it is a fact that the death penalty is used frequently in England and the homicide rate is low. But it is a fact that the death penalty is used frequently in the southern states where the homicide rate is high. There is no proof of causal connection in either case" (Sutherland, 1925). He believes that humans are gradually learning that common sense can't be a substitute for science especially in defining or implementing social policies, since contrary to common sense, science not only helps in understanding but also controlling nature of operations and procedures. Hence, the best chance of controlling any crime is to scientifically study the nature of crimes, criminals and the criminal attitudes. It is critical to analyze the physiological and social processes that are intrinsic to the criminalistic attitudes. It may turn out that the death penalty is useful for controlling crimes, and if so, it would not be because of affinity for common sense, but thorough understanding of the processes and nature of operations (Sutherland, 1925). The idea of Sutherland can be seen taken forward to conduct more of scientific research to come to any conclusion on death penalty.

Hence, different criminological literature imparts different stands supporting it with disparate rationale and scientific principles. These literature become the pedestal for shaping legal policies and the basis for court rulings.

3.2.9 Media and Death Penalty

Media mirrors the reflection of reality. Sometimes the reflection is blurred, sometimes not. In spite of that, in most of the developed and developing nations, media wields a tremendous influence on its direct as well as indirect consumers. Media represents the mood of its consumers. The rules and regulations passed as an edict by the sovereign are framed keeping in mind the larger mood of its population. The majority of population has not been in direct experience with the criminal justice system and may not understand the rationale behind the punitive policies of the government. The media helps them in formulating an opinion and articulating their viewpoints and influencing the state policies. The media acts as a link-up in pawning the opinion through print, paper, visual, and social media.

According to law professor Susan Bandes, Law and media exist in a complex feedback loop (Bandes, 2008). Visual media like Television and digital media play a pivotal role in "persuading" masses and shaping popular opinions. It not only disseminates legal information but also plays a discernible role in formulation of new rules, laws, and guidelines. Because of a strong persuasion power Television possesses, people believe everything that comes onto their screen as true and hence it directly helps in formulation of a public opinion that may lead to addition or alteration of laws.

Media brings immediate attention and addresses the cases requiring swift justice. The candle marches, solidarity petitions, celebrity interviews on crime and justice make sure that all are in unison on execution of Death Penalty or withdrawal for that matter. Debates through media channel have shown that the focus on Death Penalty has shifted its course from constitutionality, morality to efficacy. Death Penalty, once used to be norm before twentieth century has become an exception. Where lesser people used to debate in favor of removal of Death Penalty, the facts and figures show a close match between pro-abolitionist and pro-retentionist.

There is a wide spectrum of views that emerge nationally and transnationally when a gruesome and egregious case happens. Endless debates ensure questioning the relevance of death penalty. When a major chunk of the population is highlighted having a sense of fixing their wagon, appreciating, and patting the back of government for being just and strict over crime, there is another, criticizing, and highlighting the selfish motives of government behind the execution.

Cases in the past highlight how the whole life imprisonment process of the innocents has proved to be the big blot on the justice delivery system. Such cases, howsoever few in number, are capable of reversing the direction of justice. The power of media in this regard is massive.

While a section of media discusses the issue putting forward the pros and cons of the death penalty, there is another section which is more concerned with the Television Rating Point (TRP). With its constitutional right to form and express opinions/views, it is seen in many sensational cases that media steps away from reality in order to vouch for more subscribers, it started selling the story with variations/ undertones suiting the majority.

Media has been instrumental in drawing a controversial connection between sense of closure and death penalty. It popularizes, through its reach, the satisfaction that victim's loved ones get through execution. But this cannot be generalized for every victim's next of kin or general public having solidarity with victim. As per death penalty researcher Frank Zimring, "Before 1989, closure was never mentioned by the media in conjunction with capital punishment; in 1989, the two were mentioned in the same context only once" (Zimring, 2004, p. 60). However, the scenario changed since 1993 as "closure" found more frequency in the context of death penalty. In 2001 there were 500 mentions of "closure" in death penalty. As per a survey by ABC News/*Washington Post,* it was found that 60% of respondents agreed—either strongly or moderately—that death penalty was fair since it served as a closure for the kith and kin of victims (Zimring, 2004, p. 60)

The soundbite culture of media feeds on popular passions of few. Most often, the story runs in a loop with eye-catching and dramatic headlines demanding death for death, without giving due regard to socioeconomic, health or moral factors. The chronicles of the incidents are studied and broadcast. Every minute detail is collected. The result is that the least occurring crimes like murder get the most attention drawing a strong support for execution. Voices of crime survivors who are opposed to the idea of capital punishment are not appreciated and are rather silenced as it goes contrary to the expectation of masses (Hodgkinson, 2016). Media loses its objectivity when it explores the case only from an emotional angle. The case of defendant is not even considered fit for evaluation. The conundrums associated with death penalty like ethical considerations, effectiveness, need and problems of improper execution are barely discussed or deliberated upon (Bandes, 2008).

The perception of someone having committed a crime that deserves a punishment but not as severe as death penalty is too nuanced to be accepted as one. However, there have been some cases where discernible attempts to falsely convict a popular leader or person has led to decreasing support for death penalty. But the question still remains—what about the people who may commit a crime, but not "worthy of execution"? There are a few telegenic models for conveying this sort of injustice (Bandes, 2008).

Thus the media creates and feeds on fears and passions about crime that are not well linked to reality, and these fears and passions have often led to solutions poorly tailored to address the most pressing challenges of crime control and adjudication. It influences the criminal justice system at every step from formulating legislation, criminal investigation, prosecution's report to passing judicial dicta.

Media may demonize or generate empathy for an accused which may affect how the case is/was adjudicated. Cases of Karla Faye Tucker and Andrea Yates serve as good examples. Despite garnering media attention, Tucker was executed. In Yates' case, there is a notion that enormous sympathy in public eyes led to the Harris County prosecutor's unenthusiastic pursuit for capital punishment. There have always been concerns, though, about the media's biases and selective compassion playing an unwanted role of incorporating caste considerations. Unfortunately, only "certain types of emotions, and certain emotional scripts", tend to be media-friendly (Bandes, 2008).

3.3 Conclusion

Nothing has received more praise and abuse than death penalty. The chapter talks about varied non-state actors and the role they play in influencing the position of death penalty. They erect different arguments to validate their viewpoint. They function in their respective areas to achieve their objectives. However, more recently the stress is shifted more on ontological perspectives rather than just emotional appeal attached with it. The functional as well as moral argument of punishment has gained center-stage. The question raised is limited not only to death penalty and its relevance but also to the manner of its administration. These non-state actors act as a pressure group, raise emphatical arguments, garner support worldwide, and ease peaceful transitions. Death is not the best way to solve the problem of killing (Role and Responsibility of Media in Shaping Death Penalty, 2017). Although the current tide favors the abolitionist trend, not that surprisingly, there are many non-state actors who go against the historic tide of abolition. Death penalty may be too severe for some people but if the society does not inflict severe punishments, countries may run into chaos and people's lives may not be guaranteed. The chapter thus, does not negate the role of severe punishment although it does question the relevance of death penalty.

The role of each non-state actor is sui generis in the sense that although the answer may be in the form of yes or no to death penalty, yet the arguments behind it differ. The reasoning lies in history, religion, morality, statistics, ethics, human rights, deterrence, correction, economics, etc. They may not be directly involved in policy-making and penal legislations, but understating their role in influencing the death penalty will be an error of vision. The chapter has mentioned numerous examples in this behalf. I leave it to future generations to assess the role of these non-state actors keeping the geographical, political, social, economic, and legal aspects in mind. It would be a matter of interest for a future generation free of death penalty to look back and evaluate its past and analyze the role of the non-state actors.

References

ACP Group. (2003, November). *The Cotonou agreement: A user's guide for non-state actors* (pp. 31–32). Retrieved September 3, 2018, from https://ec.europa.eu/europeaid/sites/devco/files/methodology-the-cotonou-agreement-user-guide-for-non-state-actors-200311_en_2.pdf

Amnesty International. (n.d.). *Death penalty: Overview.* Retrieved September 3, 2018, from Amnesty International: https://www.amnesty.org/en/what-we-do/death-penalty/

Amnesty International. (n.d.). *Who we are.* Retrieved from https://www.amnesty.org/en/who-we-are/

Bandes, S. A. (2008). Framing wrongful convictions. Utah L. Rev., 5.

Beccaria, C. (n.d.). *On crimes and punishment.*

Beccaria, C. (1996). *On Crimes and Punishment.* New York, N.Y.: Marsilio Publishers.

Community of Sant'Egidio. (n.d.). Retrieved September 3, 2018, from https://nodeathpenalty.santegidio.org/pageID/231/langID/en/Conferences.html

Community of Sant'Egidio. (n.d.). Retrieved September 3, 2018, from https://nodeathpenalty.santegidio.org/pageID/10/Cities-for-Life.html

Community of Sant'Egidio. (n.d.). *A long path towards abolition.* Retrieved September 3, 2018, from https://nodeathpenalty.santegidio.org/pageID/225/Campaign.html

Hodgkinson, P. (2016). Juvenile death penalty in Islamic countries: The road to abolition is paved with paradox. In *Capital Punishment: New Perspectives* (pp. 80–102). Routledge.

ICDP. (n.d.). Retrieved September 3, 2018, from https://www.icomdp.org/about-icdp/

ICDP. (2018, May). *How states abolish the death penalty: 29 case-studies.* Retrieved September 3, 2018

ICDP. (n.d.). *Mandate.* Retrieved September 3, 2018, from https://www.icomdp.org/mandate/

Karn, A. (2010). Amnesty international and death penalty: Towards global abolition. In G. M. Bakken, *Invitation to an execution: A history of the death penalty in the U.S.* (p. 123). Albuquerque.

Lombroso, C., Gibson, M., & Rafter, N. H. (2006). Criminal man, translated and with a new introduction.

Member Organisations. (n.d.). Retrieved August 27, 2018, from WCADP: https://www.worldcoalition.org/Member-organizations.html

OCHCR. (n.d.). *UN Human Rights chief calls on Indonesia to stop executions.* Retrieved September 3, 2018, from OCHCR: https://www.ohchr.org/EN/NewsEvents/Pages/DisplayNews.aspx?NewsID=20305&LangID=E

OCHR. (2016). *Death Penalty and the Victims.* (I. Šimonovi´c, Ed.) New York. Retrieved September 3, 2018, from https://www.ohchr.org/EN/newyork/Documents/Death-Penalty-and-the-Victims-WEB.PDF

OHCHR. (2014). *Moving away from the death penalty: Arguments, trends and perspectives.* (I. Šimonovi´c, Ed.) New York. Retrieved September 3, 2018, from https://www.ohchr.org/Lists/MeetingsNY/Attachments/52/Moving-Away-from-the-Death-Penalty.pdf

OHCHR. (n.d.). *Death penalty.* Retrieved September 3, 2018, from United Nations Human Rights—Office of the High Commissioner: https://www.ohchr.org/EN/Issues/DeathPenalty/Pages/DPIndex.aspx

Plaçais, E. G. (2016, December 20). *The UN General Assembly voted overwhelmingly for a 6th resolution calling for a universal moratorium on executions.* Retrieved September 3, 2018, from WCADP: https://www.worldcoalition.org/The-UN-General-Assembly-voted-overwhelmingly-for-a-6th-resolution-calling-for-a-universal-moratorium-on-executions.html

Radelet, M. L., & Akers, R. L. (1996). Deterrence and the death penalty: The views of the experts. *Journal of Criminal Law & Criminology*, *87*, 1.

Radelet, M. L., & Bedau, H. A. (1998). The execution of the innocent. *Law and Contemporary Problems*, *61*(4), 105–124.

Role and responsibility of media in shaping death penalty (2017, October 16). Retrieved September 3, 2018, from UK Essays: https://www.ukessays.com/essays/media/role-responsibility-media-shaping-death-7565.php

Sant'Egidio. (2018, April 10). The African turning point: to humanise prisons and to abolish the Death Penalty. CÔTE D'IVOIRE. Retrieved September 3, 2018, from https://www.santegidio.org/pageID/30284/langID/en/itemID/25024/The-African-turning-point-to-humanise-prisons-and-to-abolish-the-Death-Penalty.html

Schuessler, K. (1952). The deterrent influence of the death penalty. *The Annals of the American Academy of Political and Social Science, 284*, 54–62. Retrieved from https://www.jstor.org/stable/1029443

Sellin, T. (1959). The death penalty. Philadelphia, Penn.: The American Law Institute (1967. Capital Punishment).

Sutherland, E. (1925). Murder and the death penalty. *Journal of the American Institute of Criminal Law and Criminology, 15*(4), 522–529. https://doi.org/10.2307/1134522.

UN. (2004, June 21). Press Release. *United Nations urged to pay more heed to role of 'Non-State Actors' in approach to global problems*. Retrieved September 5, 2018, from https://www.un.org/press/en/2004/sg2089.doc.htm

UNRIC. (2012, November 21). *Ban welcomes General Assembly committee's record vote on death penalty moratorium*. Retrieved September 3, 2018, from United Nations Regional Information Centre for Western Europe: https://www.unric.org/en/latest-un-buzz/28048-ban-welcomes-general-assembly-committees-record-vote-on-death-penalty-moratorium

WCADP. (n.d.). *Worldwide database*. Retrieved September 3, 2018, from https://www.worldcoalition.org/worldwide-database.html

World Coalition against the Death Penalty. (2017, October 10). Death Penalty and Poverty. *Poverty and justice: A deadly mix. Mobilisation Kit*. Retrieved September 3, 2018

Zavatta, L. (2017, June). Controversial theories on the death penalty. *Scientific Research, 8*(2). 1.4236/blr.2017.82012

Zimring, F. E. (2004). *The contradictions of American capital punishment*. Oxford University Press.

Chapter 4
Public Opinion on Death Penalty

4.1 Introduction

Michel Foucault, one of the greatest philosophers of the twentieth century, talked about the disappearance of punishment as a public spectacle in Chap. 1 of his book *Discipline and Punish: The Birth of the Prison (1975).* The chapter opens with a passage that describes the execution of a man for committing parricide. The flesh from his body was torn, subsequent to which molten lead, burning oil, and boiling wax were poured onto him while his body was being tugged by horses and consumed by fire. Regardless of the nature of the crime, such modes of punishment were frequent in the seventeenth and eighteenth centuries. However, toward the start of the nineteenth century the "*gloomy festival of punishment started dying out*" (Foucault, 1975, p. 8).

Foucault notes a shift from punishment on the "body" to the "soul." The ignominy received by the offender from the pubic gradually transformed into pity and sympathy. Psychological aspects of a crime took upon great importance, such as the relations between the criminal, his past and his crime. The public attitude was leaning toward implementation of sentences that had the potential to ameliorate the offender rather than merely torture him. The nineteenth century did not just mark a decline in public spectacle, but also a decline on the hold of the body. A whole new humanitarian perspective came about that highlighted the importance of moral rights in penal measures. In the words of Foucault, "*Execution was meant to affect life rather than the body*" (Foucault, 1975, p. 12).

As is evident from Foucault's works, public opinion has greatly influenced and shaped the decisions of the ruling class in matters concerning punishments for the offender. Public opinion reveals popular thinking on a particular political issue in a given region; it is the collective opinion of the people in a society on a given problem (Dugger, n.d.). Public opinion has always and still continues to play an important part in the debate on death penalty. It is so paramount that all three organs of the government, namely, the executive, legislature, and judiciary, attach a great amount of weight to it in the creation, enforcement, and implementation of laws around the issue of death penalty (Vidmar & Ellsworth, 1974).

S. P. Sahni and M. Junnarkar, *The Death Penalty*,
https://doi.org/10.1007/978-981-15-3129-3_4

In this chapter, the author seeks to analyze public opinion on capital punishment across several countries all over the globe. The author will further examine the factors that aid the public in coming to their decision. Two more important aspects that the author will be touching upon is the role of the media in influencing the public opinion and the impact of these polls on judicial decision-making.

4.2 Public Opinion Polls and Judicial Decision-Making

4.2.1 Africa

In Africa, some methods employed to enforce capital punishment include firing squad, hanging, and in certain Muslim states such as northern Nigeria and Sudan, even stoning to death for certain offences is common practice (www.deathpenaltyworldwide.com). In some instances, executions have been carried out in public on the belief that "it is a fitting terror to the masses, and it is a comforting sight to the family and friends of the victim" (Working Group on the Death Penalty in Africa, 2011). Out of 54 states in the African Union, 18 have abolished death penalty and 19 no longer execute convicts. However, the retentionists contend that the government cannot ignore the strong support of public opinion on capital punishment (Zitren, 2015). In 1996, a survey found that 71.4% of the people in South Africa favored the death penalty (Human Sciences Research Council, 1996). In 2004, a poll was carried out to find out whether the public wanted to reinstate the death penalty of which 90% were in favor (Chenwi, 2005).

A survey was adopted to obtain a sample of 104 people in Cape Town, the legislative capital of South Africa in which 59.6% of the people favored the retention of death penalty and 40.4% favored abolition. Among the retentionists were more than one-half of men (while no less than two-third women), people from the older generation, the ones not educated beyond high school, owners of business, white-collar workers, and the Catholics and Protestants, citing their reasons to be that an eye for an eye (referring to the text of the Bible) serves to deter crime and the alternative of holding offenders in prison eats into taxpayers' money. Among the abolitionists were the younger generation, the well educated who attended college and university and the Jews, citing their reasons to be that the death penalty is against the fundamental notions of ethics and morality due to its cruel nature, it does not deter crime and the possibility of convicting an innocent is extremely high (Midgley, 1974).

While in Ghana, a survey was conducted to obtain a random sample of 2460 people by the Centre for Criminology and Criminal Justice. It found that majority of Ghanians are opposed to capital punishment with a high 61.7% support abolition and a meager 39.3% oppose abolition (Tankebe & Boakye, 2016). People between the ages of 18 and 24 and those educated till only high school showed the highest opposition to death penalty. People between the ages of 45 and 54 and those with higher levels of education showed a higher support for death penalty. In the category of religion, support for death penalty was found to be weakest among Catholics, Protestants, and Muslims. Crimes such as armed robbery and rape of a child below 10 years gained highest support for imposition of death penalty, whereas stealing of public funds and causing financial loss to state gained minimal support (Tankebe, Boakye, & Atupare, 2015).

Africa has one of the lowest execution rates in comparison to the rest of the world. Nearly 80% countries in Africa have abolished the death penalty, with only a meager 10 countries actually enforcing executions in the past decade. Only 24 executions were carried out in 2018 in 4 of the 31 countries that retain the death penalty in sub-Saharan Africa, 2 of them in Botswana, 13 in Somalia, approximately 7 in South Sudan, and 2 in Sudan. As recently as 2013, there had been 64 executions in five countries, nearly all of them in Somalia and Sudan. Botswana saw only one execution in 2013, only three between 1987 and 2006 and then at least one a year since, except 2011 (Blok & Suter, 2017).

Several factors triggered off the abolition of capital punishment in Africa. In South Africa, the end of apartheid was a direct mark of abolition. Death penalty was held to be violative of the right to life, dignity, equality, and freedom from inhumane, degrading, or cruel treatment as envisaged under their Constitution. Namibia too, after becoming independent from South Africa, abolished the death penalty in an attempt to banning the arbitrary and repressive use of such techniques that were prevalent during the apartheid colonial period. Mozambique and Angola were faced with a different scenario as they did not suffer from any prevalent capital punishment under the Portuguese rule. Both these countries, however, introduced the death penalty following their independence only to abolish it again 20 years later. The reason for this was that both these countries were faced with civil war post-independence. One of the "tools of political oppression" used in the war was the death penalty, thereby, in turn, making the abolition of the same essential to their peace settlements (Blok & Suter, 2017).

In *Republic v. Mbushuu and Another, (1994) 2 LRC 335*, the Tanzanian High Court had to decide on the constitutionality of the death penalty. After it was pointed out that the majority of people in Tanzania supported death penalty, the Court held: "It is our decided opinion that what measures are necessary to deter the commission of capital crimes or to protect society are matters for decision by every individual society … the crucial question is whether the death penalty is reasonably necessary to protect the right to life. For this, we say it is the society, which decides. The trial judge in the above passage acknowledges that presently the society deems the death penalty as reasonably necessary. So, we find that the death penalty is not arbitrary and it is reasonably necessary."

This issue of validity of public opinion on death penalty in judicial decision-making came up for consideration in the case of *S v. Makwanyane, 1995 (3) SA 391*. The question was not what majority of South Africans found to be a favorable punishment for murder, it was whether the constitution permitted it. The court on this point found that "while public opinion may have some relevance, it is not a substitute for the duty vested in the Court to uphold the provisions of the Constitution." While the rejection of public opinion is to be confined to narrow limits, the court held that "only when public opinion does not accord with standards of civilization will it be rejected outright." The court must determine "how much of the public opinion is relevant and what weight can be attached to it in assessing the constitutionality of a provision" (Zlotnick, 1996).

4.2.2 America

As of 2017, capital punishment is legal in 31 out of 50 US states (N.A., 2017a). While the most frequently employed method for death penalty in America is by use of the lethal injection, several states have adopted other methods as well such as electrocution, gas, firing squad, and hanging (Cornell Centre on Death Penalty Worldwide, 2014). The constitutionality of lethal injection has been in question due to its several failed attempts at carrying out executions in the expected manner. The substances used in lethal injections have been continuously changed from time to time due to their inefficiency. In 2014, Dennis McGuire was executed for the murder of a pregnant woman through lethal injection by the State of Ohio. He took 25 min to die after making loud snorting noises. His children and daughter-in-law witnessed this event (Hummer, 2014). In another incident in 2014, Michael Lee Wilson was executed via lethal injection by the State of Oklahoma, wherein he stated, "I feel my whole body burning" after he had been injected. It was revealed later on that the likelihood of Oklahoma having used an expired supply of drugs was very high. The opponents of death penalty believe that this method of execution causes tremendous pain and suffering to the prisoners thereby violating the constitutional mandate of "cruel and unusual punishment" (Cornell Centre on Death Penalty Worldwide, 2014).

According to the 2017 Gallup Poll, while America still stands in favor of the death penalty, the number of people supporting it has massively dropped. From its peak at 80% in 1997, it has reached an all-time low support at merely 55% in 2017. From a sample size of 1028 people, a survey of the nation revealed that 41% of the population opposed the death penalty in 2017 compared to a meager 16% in 1997. When posed the question of what one would choose in between death penalty and life imprisonment, 50% favored the former, 45% favored the latter, and 5% had no opinion. Looking at these figures, it appears that America will soon reach the state of equilibrium between the advocates and the critics of capital punishment (Gallup Poll, 2017).

The reasons given by the proponents of death penalty include: an eye for an eye, saves taxpayer's money, sets an example for the society, offenders cannot be rehabilitated, beneficial to the victim and the victim's family, and relieves prison overcrowding. The reasons given by the opponents of death penalty include: it is wrong to take a life, persons may be wrongly convicted, punishment must be left to God, offenders must be made to suffer and think about their crime, does not deter crime and there is a possibility of rehabilitation of the offender (Gallup Poll, 2017).

Another survey conducted on sample size of 1000 people classifies them into different categories of gender, age, race, and family income to analyze their support/opposition toward death penalty. The survey revealed that Whites, males, those above the age of 45, with a high-income level are more likely to support the death penalty in comparison to Blacks/Hispanics, females, those below the age of 45, with a low-income level. The survey further revealed that the support for capital punishment is higher among Republicans than Democrats and independents. Most people in favor of the death penalty felt that it should be carried out as quick and painless as possible. Some of the reasons indicating high support toward death penalty included making sure that justice is served, deterring others from breaking the law, and giving closure to the victims' families (YouGov Survey, 2015).

A survey via face-to-face interviews was carried out on a sample size of 1000 people in Trinidad to ascertain their support for mandatory death penalty for murder. Professor Roger Hood of Oxford University and Dr. Florence Seemungal, a psychologist from Trinidad, designed the survey, which was further commissioned by the Death Penalty Project in London. Ninety-one percent people showed support toward death penalty while 9% wished for its abolition. However, 64% of them preferred to opt for a discretionary death penalty to mandatory death penalty. The main reasons given by the retentionists of capital punishment included retribution. 87% of the people said that they would support capital punishment even if evidence showed that life imprisonment proved to be a better deterrent than the latter (Hood & Seemungal, 2011).

In the case of *Stanford v. Kentucky, 491 U.S. 361 (1989)*, the US Supreme Court was faced with the question of whether a death sentence could be imposed on the 17-year-old Kevin Stanford for murder and rape. The court held that capital punishment could be imposed on any person who is above the age of 16 years and this does not amount to "cruel and unusual punishment" as envisaged under the eighth amendment. On March 1, 2005, a change was brought about in the law wherein the United States Supreme Court ruled that capital punishment for those below the age of 18 is unconstitutional.

In the case of *Weems v. United States, 217 U.S. 349 (1910)*, the Supreme Court held that "cruel and unusual punishment" under the eighth amendment may change as "public opinion becomes enlightened by a human justice." Subsequently, in *Trop v. Dulles, 356 U.S. 86 (1958)*, the court stated that the eighth amendment derived its meaning of the words "cruel and unusual punishment" from the "evolving standards of decency that mark the progress of a maturing society." Finally, in the case of *Furman v. Georgia, 408 U.S. 238 (1972)*, the US Supreme Court held that the death penalty violated the eighth amendment prohibition of "cruel and unusual" punishment. The meaning of "cruel and unusual punishment" extends to a direct assessment of the values of the society at large. While the ruling in *Furman* reaffirmed its precedents, both the concurring and dissenting judges "expressed sharp disagreement on the question of where the public stands on the issue of capital punishment, whether opinion polls are valid indicators of public opinion about capital punishment and the extent to which enlightened public opinion determines contemporary standards of decency" (Vidmar & Ellsworth, 1974).

Furman discussed the value and weightage that must be afforded to public opinion on capital punishment. Firstly, this case rejected the discretionary application of death penalty. In other words, if the public favors the death penalty in a way that would lead to an "arbitrary imposition of capital punishment," the judiciary would not accept such opinions. Secondly, Justice Marshall, in his concurring opinion, stated, "Law should be guided only by informed public opinion as it is not possible to determine whether capital punishment as it actually functions offends a person's sense of decency; if that person is ignorant or misinformed about capital punishment." He also stated that knowledge about the "psychological and physical realities of the death penalty" is an important factor that influences public opinion. Only when the public is aware of these realities can their opinion be held acceptable. Thirdly, public opinion that is inconsistent with the fundamental provisions of the Constitution will not hold a very high value as compared to those that are compatible with Constitutional provisions. Fourthly, public opinion based on discrimination against sex, race, gender, class, etc. will hold no value and cannot be a "standard to judge public morality." Furthermore, public opinion favoring the death penalty out of "retribution and vengeance" is not conclusive and thereby cannot be relied upon. Lastly, support for death penalty can vary at different degrees. Thus, support for capital punishment at a more "general or abstract level" will not be given much weightage, whereas support in more "concrete situations" will be given higher weightage (Vidmar & Ellsworth, 1974).

The ruling of *Furman* gave rise to discontent among supporters of the death penalty. The court, however, did not leave the supporters without any remedy. In the case of *Gregg v. Georgia, 428 U.S. 153, 155 (1976)*, the court ruled that capital punishment would be implemented provided two procedural safeguards are met. First, execution is to be permitted only for the most severe crimes, which are to be termed as "capital offences." Second, after the jury comes to a conclusion that "sufficient aggravating circumstances exist," the judges will be permitted to impose the death penalty. Soon after this ruling, capital punishment was reinstated in more than 30 states in America for murder and other crimes (Markowitz & Harver, 2003).

4.2.3 Australia

Capital punishment had been consistently practiced in all Australian states until 51 years ago when Australia saw its last execution. In 1967, Ronald Ryan Joseph was executed in Melbourne for shooting a prison guard during an attempted escape from a prison in Victoria (York, 2017). What made this incident unique was the protests and demonstrations that broke out across the nation wherein people demanded for the abolition of capital punishment, public gatherings took place outside the prison where Ryan was to be hanged, the media's widespread reporting on this incident that grabbed the attention of the public, and lastly, Henry Edward Bolt, an Australian politician's determination to have him hanged. Due to the lack of evidence presented by the Crown as to who fired the shot, the public expected his death sentence to be reduced to life imprisonment at the least.

There had been a heavy decline in the support for death penalty. Furthermore, since 1951, all the death sentences in Victoria had been commuted (Muir, 2017). Finally, in 1973, the Parliament of Australia passed the Death Penalty Abolition Act to abolish capital punishment under the laws of Commonwealth. To ensure strict compliance with this, the Crimes Legislation Amendment (Torture Prohibition and Death Penalty Abolition) Act 2010 was introduced which barred any state in Australia from reintroducing capital punishment (United Nations, 2014).

As per a poll carried out by Roy Morgan in December 2005, two-third of the Australian population believed that the punishment for people convicted of murder should be imprisonment and not capital punishment (Death Penalty Information Centre, n.d.). Another survey was conducted via face-to-face interviews and questionnaires in both rural and urban areas. The study revealed that a total of 59% of the sample of 3012 people were in support of the death penalty for persons convicted of murder, 26% opposed it. Women were found to be less supportive of capital punishment than men; however, the difference was only of 4%. The older showed no difference in support than the younger and income showed no correlation to support for death penalty once demographic differences were accounted for (e.g., difference in education). Married persons were 5% more supportive of the death penalty than the unmarried. The more educated people were less supportive of death penalty. Religion had no impact on support for death penalty. People who watched a lot of television showed support for death penalty (Kelley & Braithwaite, 1990).

The Prime Minister of Australia in 2006 stated that he was happy with death penalty stance taken by Australia because "the law can make mistakes" (N.A., The Age, 2006). The 2002 Bali Bombing further influenced Australia's decision to abolish capital punishments wherein one of the perpetrators when questioned about the prospects of capital punishment stated, "It will be a martyr's death and that is what I am looking for" (Goodsir, 2003). Australia believes that terrorists are not afraid of the death penalty. Rather, the possibility of being given capital punishment acts as an incentive for them to commit crimes (Australian Human Rights Commission, 2006). The death penalty in Australia was abolished to respect the sanctity of human life. Australia having ratified the Second Optional Protocol on the International Covenant on Civil and Political Rights (ICCPR) is committed toward the abolition of death penalty as stated in its preamble.

4.2.4 Asia

While Asia has shown increasing movement toward abolition of capital punishment, it still stands to be the highest executer in the world. However, there has been a shift back toward death penalty due to increased terrorist attacks, rape, and offences related to drugs and narcotic substances. In 2016, nearly 160 executions have been carried out across 11 countries in Asia (Lane, 2015).

Although Pakistan's execution rate has reduced over the years, it accounts for 87% of the executions in Asia. The data on China, which is believed to be the world's top executioner with its figures crossing thousands of people each year, is nowhere to be found. Taiwan carried out an execution on a person merely 3 weeks after his death sentence was announced. Bangladesh, Malaysia, and Afghanistan hanged ten, nine, and eight people, respectively, in 2016. Indonesia and Singapore carried out capital punishment on four people in 2016 of which three were foreigners. Japan implemented the death penalty on three people in 2016 of which one was a woman (N.A., The Nation, 2017b). While Nepal, Bhutan, and Sri Lanka have abolished the death penalty, the rest of South Asia has not (Jha, 2017). India has carried out only four executions in the last two decades of which three were for involvement in terrorist activities (N.A., India Today, 2015). A report by Amnesty International, an organization focused on human rights, revealed that Pakistan and Bangladesh executed more than 220 people and Vietnam over 130 people in 2013. This report further revealed that China and North Korea exceeded 1000 people though exact figures were nowhere to be found.

In 2009, Malaysia's representative at Geneva expressed to the United Nations Human Rights Council about its considerations of replacing death penalty with life imprisonment in Malaysia. However, he made it conspicuous that this cannot be achieved without public support. It is in this backdrop that a survey via face-to-face interviews of 1535 people was conducted in 2012 to ascertain whether Malaysia shows support for abolition of death penalty. The survey, which was backed by reputed institutions such as Bar Council of Malaysia and Malaysian Human Rights Commission, revealed that a large majority of the sample (which was inclusive of both Malaysians and non-Malaysians) showed support for death penalty, whether mandatory or discretionary. Support for capital punishment was the highest at 91%, for one of the five drug trafficking offences between 74 and 80% and firearms offences at 83%. Those supporting the death penalty cited their two main reasons to be that everyone found guilty deserves to die and it serves as a tool for deterrence of crime (Hood, 2013).

Japan has often been referred to as one of the safest countries in the world as crime rates in Japan have remained relatively low. Presently, there are 18 offences in Japan, which are punishable with the death penalty. However, in practice, capital punishment has primarily been imposed for crimes relating to murder. In 2010, the Cabinet Office released the results of a public opinion poll about the justice system around the issue of death penalty. The people taking the survey were given three options to choose from: (1) The death penalty should be abolished unconditionally, (2) In some cases, the death penalty cannot be avoided, and (3) I don't know/it depends. The survey showed that 85.6% of the people picked option 2. Among these, 54% people stated that this system is required in order to do justice to the victim/victim's family and 51.5% believed that this would help deter violent crimes (Tagusari, 2010).

As discussed above, in spite of China being the highest executioner in the world, there appears to be very little data available on the executions carried out in that country. In order to ascertain the public opinion of capital punishment in China, Oberwittler and Qin from the Max Planck Institute in Freiburg conducted 4472 face-to-face interviews in Beijing, Hubei, and Guangdong between 2007 and 2008. However, the survey revealed that only 26% of the people were interested in the issue of death penalty, whereas the remaining 74% were not interested or did not know anything about death penalty. Looking at this, they concluded that public opinion is not a major influence on the execution rates in the region (Zimring & Johnson, 2012). Another survey that was conducted online revealed that the support for death penalty in China had massively dropped from 95% in 1995 to 17% in 2003. However, in 2008, this support jumped up to 34%. People who took this survey believed that China ought to reduce its use of capital punishment especially for non-violent crimes (Zhang, 2014).

In India, the death penalty follows the "rarest of rare" doctrine. This means that it is only in the rarest of rare cases that the offender will be given a capital punishment. In 2013, a survey of 20,000 people across 267 constituencies in 18 states was conducted by the Centre for the Study of Developing Societies (CSDS) as part of the CNN-IBN-The Hindu Election Tracker. This survey found that 40% of the people believed that death penalty should be replaced with life imprisonment (Live Law Research Team, 2016). Another survey carried out on a sample size of 200 revealed that 104 people favored the death penalty, 80 opposed it, and 16 had no response. 84% of the 104 people supported the death penalty in cases of murder and rape, whereas 64% of the 104 people believed that it should be imposed on women and juvenile in cases of heinous crimes. Decreasing crime rates, victim satisfaction, and deterrent effect were some of the reasons that gained public support toward the implementation of capital punishment (Choudhri & Hiremath, n.d.).

The Supreme Court of India, in the case of *Bachan Singh v. State of Punjab, (1980) 2 SCC 684*, cited the United States Supreme Court ruling of *Furman* to show that judges are ill-equipped to capture public opinion. The court stated, "rejection by the people of the approach adopted in Furman furnishes proof that judicial opinion does not necessarily reflect the moral attitudes of the people. At the same time, it is a reminder that Judges should not take upon themselves the responsibility of becoming oracles or spokesmen of public opinion … leave the function of assessing public opinion to the chosen representatives of the people in the legislature concerned." The court upheld the constitutionality of the death penalty but confined its application to the rarest of rare cases to reduce arbitrariness.

The matter come up for consideration in the case of *Santosh Kumar Satishbhushan v. State of Maharashtra, (2009) 6 SCC 498*, wherein the court while citing *Bachan Singh* held, "It is also to be pointed out that public opinion is difficult to fit in the rarest of rare matrix. People's perception of crime is neither an objective circumstance relating to crime nor to the criminal. Perception of public is extraneous to conviction as also sentencing, at least in capital sentencing, according to the mandate of Bachan Singh. Rarest of rare policy and legislative policy on death punishment may not be essentially tuned to public opinion. We are governed by the dictum of Bachan Singh (supra) according to which life imprisonment is the rule and death punishment is an exception."

No discussion on the validity of capital punishment in India can be complete without going through the fine details of the Law Commission Reports. The Law

Commission of India (1967) in Report No. 35 on "The Death Penalty," in its recommendations said: "*It is difficult to rule out the validity of, or the strength behind, many of the arguments for abolition. Nor does the Commission treat lightly the argument of irrevocability of the sentence of death, the need for a modern approach, the severity of capital punishment, and the strong feeling shown by certain sections of* ***public opinion****, in stressing deeper questions of human values. Having regard, however, to the conditions in India, to the variety of the social upbringing of its inhabitants, to the disparity in the level of morality and education in the country, to the vastness of its area, to the diversity of its population, and to the paramount need for maintaining law and order in the country at the present juncture, India cannot risk the experiment of abolition of capital punishment.*"

4.2.5 Europe

Except Belarus, every European country has abolished capital punishment. Belarus has executed over 200 people since the 1990s. The last two executions that took place in Belarus were in 2017 (Smith, 2018). In 2012, Latvia becomes the last European Union Member State to abolish capital punishment. The primary reason for a large part of Europe being free from death penalty is that abolishing capital punishment is an explicit and absolute condition precedent for membership in the European Union because "it is incompatible with human rights, violates human dignity, does not deter crime and it is an inhuman, degrading and irreversible punishment" (Delegation of the European Union to the Council of Europe, 2017c). Furthermore, Protocol No. 6 of the European Convention of Human Rights calls for a complete abolition on the use of death penalty.

A survey carried out on a sample size of 1100 in Belarus with the financial support of the European Union revealed that public opinion on the issue of capital punishment was divided among both proponents and opponents of capital punishment. When directly asked about abolition of death penalty, 63.8% supported capital punishment. However, the public opinion showed a specific trend between the categories of age and religion. Those between the ages of 18 and 29 were less supportive of capital punishment than those above 30. Those that believed in God opposed the death penalty whereas the non-believers supported capital punishment. The main reasons that gained support for capital punishment were safety concerns and an eye-for-an-eye principle. This argument was, however, primarily common around women, older generation, and those living in provinces. The main reasons that gained support for abolition of death penalty were sanctity of human life and imperfections in the judicial system leaving the possibility of convicting an innocent (Penal Reform International, 2013).

The Murder (Abolition of Death Penalty) Act 1965 was introduced to replace capital punishment with life imprisonment in the United Kingdom. The ratification of the European Convention on Human Rights further secured the future commitment toward abolition of death penalty in the UK of which Protocol 13 abolished "capital punishment in all circumstances" (Death Penalty Information Centre, n.d.). Votes have been held every year to examine whether the public wants it to be restored. In 1983, when the annual survey began, the British Social Attitudes survey revealed that support for death penalty was at 75%. In 1995, when the Parliament debated the restoration of death penalty, it was found that 76% of the British were in support of this proposition (*ibid.*). Even after the referendum which ended in support for Brexit, the support for death penalty still stands. The YouGov survey revealed that more than half of the people wanted the death penalty to be reinstated at a support of 53% (Kentish, 2017).

4.3 Analysis of Public Opinion Polls

4.3.1 Survey Questions and Demographic Variables

As we studied above, each country uses different methods to determine whether the public opinion is in favor of the death penalty. "A single question is a poor measure of support because it fails to capture the complexities that should be considered in evaluating death penalty attitudes" (Applegate, Wright, Dunaway, Cullen & Wooldredge, 1993). Willingness to use capital punishment also varies depending on the severity of the crime and the characteristic of the criminal in question (Ellsworth & Ross, 1983). Support for death penalty in cases of the criminal being mentally handicapped, a female or a juvenile is low (Vito & Kiel, 1998). Simple yes/no questions fail to capture the thought process behind reaching such conclusions (Ellsworth & Ross, 1983).

Demographic variables are the most common method adopted to show a difference in support for the death penalty. These variables include sex, age, income, etc. Sex indicates a support for capital punishment among men. This is sometimes misconstrued as an opposition to capital punishment among women. However, this distinction is just a matter of degree and not opposition wherein there is a higher degree of support among males than females for capital punishment. In fact, some studies show that sex has no nexus with punitivity at all (Sato, 2014). The age factor indicates that older people are more likely to support the death penalty than the young. There is also evidence suggesting that persons with lower levels of education and higher levels of income support death penalty. These two elements are in direct contradiction with each other, as those with higher incomes tend to have higher levels of education (Sato, 2014). Further, religion "can be a source of punitive or more progressive views" depending on how religion is interpreted by the individual (Unnever, Cullen & Applegate, 2005). From the very fact that White people support the death penalty more than the Black people shows that "support for death penalty stems from racial prejudice ... the opinion polls exaggerate legitimate support for capital punishment" (Barkan & Cohn, 2005).

Demographic variables are not entirely sufficient in explaining public support for death penalty. They have less explanatory value than symbolic or instrumental factors (Sato, 2014). Instrumental factors are linked to the desire at lower crime levels. People who fear crime believe that employing harsher punishments can reduce crime. Symbolic factors are those that link a person's support for death penalty to their "social and political values" (Tyler and Weber, 1982). Therefore, symbolic factors signify an individual's "deeply held beliefs and values" and instrumental factors are "logical, rational purposes often serving utilitarian functions" (Vollum & Buffington-Vollum, 2010).

4.3.2 Creating Specific Scenarios

Merely noting general levels of support in favor of or in opposition to death penalty will not give us the type of data needed to judge what the public really wants with respect to capital punishment. To reach this conclusion, it is essential that we take into account the vantage point toward capital punishment in light of "specific types of criminals for specific crimes and under specific circumstances" (Vidmar & Ellsworth, 1974).

As discussed above, the approach to collect public opinion on death penalty must not be of a very general character. In 1973, the Minnesota Poll asked people whether the death penalty should be made mandatory for four types of crimes. Fifty-nine percent people were in agreement for a situation where a kidnapper or hijacker kills a person, 58% for assassination of federal official, 49% for murder of a law enforcement officer, and 39% for crimes against the federal government such as treason, sabotage, and espionage (Minnesota Poll, Minneapolis, 1973). This poll helped gage the public support for death penalty for specific types of crimes. While such a study is concise to some extent, as the questions are not too wide, there are still certain elements left unaddressed. One aspect that would strengthen this poll would be to define the term mandatory as the view of the public is subject to change depending on the facts and circumstances of each case.

The best way to judge whether a person support or oppose the death penalty would be to put forth a hypothetical scenario before him/her. The base scenario can then be arranged in several different permutations and combinations in order to see whether public opinion changes with minor changes to the facts of a case. For example, if there is a law stating that any act by one person which leads to the death of another will be punishable by death penalty, in which of the following scenarios should A, a thief be executed for shooting and resulting in the death of B, a policeman:

1. A, who had just stolen jewellery worth Rs. 5 crore was walking in a park when he had an encounter with B. B asked A to surrender for the theft committed by him, to which A agreed. Even after A handed over the stolen jewellery and surrendered himself, B started beating him up. B continued beating him up for

20 min until A started bleeding from many parts of his body. Unable to bear the brunt of the beatings, A took out his revolver and shot B dead.

2. A was walking in a park when B mistakenly attacked him instead of attacking the actual thief C. When B pointed his gun at A and threatened to fire, A snatched the gun from B and shot him, resulting in his death.
3. A was walking in a park while B was searching for the actual thief C. B upon seeing C's 5-year-old child who was also walking in the park, grabbed him by the collar and started beating up the child. B then called up C for him to hear the cries of his child. Upon seeing this, A took out his gun and shot B dead in order to protect the child.

Like the above combinations from the base fact, many more combinations can be created to give to the public several different and alternative scenarios. By presenting to the public a wide range of such scenarios, it helps to determine where their opinion really lies and whether a small additional fact in a case can impact their opinion on whether to grant the accused the death penalty or not. To much surprise, even those people who had vehemently advocated for death penalty can be swayed from their stance by a small change in any factual matter in a given case. Thus, the idea of presenting before the public many hypothetical scenarios, like the ones listed above, is extremely vital and conclusive in determining public support for capital punishment.

4.3.3 Uninformed Decisions

A general understanding according to the population of what capital punishment entails will give us an idea of whether the public is aware of the nitty-gritty involved in carrying out such executions. From the polls above, we have seen that people often support the death penalty on the belief that it deters crime and saves the taxpayers' money that goes into holding prisoners in jail for long periods of time. However, if there was a good reason to doubt these assumptions would the public opinion change? Furthermore, the "physical and psychological realities of executions" can turn out to be so devastating to some people that they might want to take a more humanitarian approach as suggested by Foucault (Vidmar & Ellsworth, 1974). To put it simply, the level of awareness generated among the public with regard to the "humanitarian" and "utilitarian" aspects of death penalty is the stepping-stone to understanding the public opinion on capital punishment.

4.3.4 Size and Polling Areas

Another limitation duly noted in all the surveys taken is the sample size and polling areas chosen for conducting the same. Some of the largest samples taken in a survey for gathering the public opinion on death penalty have been seen to cover around 3000–4000 persons. In this paper itself, the study with the largest sample size analyzed was the one carried out by Oberwittler and Qin from the Max Planck Institute in Freiburg that covered 4472 persons. While this number is vast, it is not conclusive of the views of the general public because a few thousand people cannot be said to represent the views of the entire nation. This is where most surveys fall short as they are restricted to only a very miniscule part of the population and thereby cannot encapsulate enough data to reflect the opinion of an entire country. Apart from inadequately representing majority of the country, polling results are also usually confined to a specific area/town. Due to this, the type and class of persons that are being surveyed are also one of a kind. This confinement is interlinked with biases that exist in formation of opinions on a given subject matter. For example, public opinion is often biased being based on gender roles, sex, religion, caste, etc. Minorities of Black people among a majority of White people are less likely to support the death penalty due to factors such as racism. Wealthier people are more likely to support the death penalty as compared to the impoverished due to their abundant access to legal resources (Vidmar & Ellsworth, 1974). No number of polls can ever be conclusive until all these discrepancies are removed from the study.

4.3.5 Public Education: A Better Alternative?

One of the main reasons that countries retain or abolish capital punishment is deeply rooted in the public support or opposition toward this practice. However, as noted above, opinion polls are influenced by a range of factors and thereby more often than not lead to inaccurate conclusions. One of the many and most primary factors is making uninformed decisions due to a lack of knowledge and information about the subject matter. This would logically conclude that public education efforts to make the public more aware of the realities that are involved in carrying out capital punishments would be more productive than carrying out opinion polls on uniformed persons. The best way to impart public education would be through the media, such as newspapers, magazines, television, radio, social networking sites, etc., since it has the ability to reach the bulk of the population (Blok & Suter, 2017). In Malawi, one of the television channels aired a documentary about a death row prisoner, Byson Kaula, who was freed from prison and later went on to become a teacher. This documentary was well received by the public with many giving their approval to the alternative of rehabilitation (Mana, 2016). Another Canadian television channel covered the case of a 14-year-old man named Steven Truscott, who was wrongly sentenced to death penalty. As a result, the public demanded his acquittal and also saw a larger change in the mindset with majority of them campaigning for abolition of capital punishment (Strange, 2018). Similar was the public wave after the media reported the mishandled and careless execution of Clayton Lockett in 2014, which was regarded as a cruel and unusual punishment (Stern, 2015).

Apart from using the media as a way to educate the public on the realities behind carrying out executions, several other methods can be adopted. In many parts of the world, especially in countries like India where religion is given so much importance, religious institutions and leaders play a vital role in influencing the ideologies of any class of people holding that specific set of religious beliefs. They not only have reached to a wide number of people in the country, but also spread their message to their followers on religious, moral, spiritual, and humanitarian values of life as would be permissible within the four corners of their religion. In Zimbabwe, 23% of the Senate is formed by religious leaders who unanimously ruled out death penalty in 2016. Similarly, in Zambia, the Council of Churches have strongly advocated for the abolition of capital punishment, thereby largely influencing the general public especially followers of their religion (Blok & Suter, 2017). In Botswana, there exists a human rights group that goes by the name DITSHWANELO, which educates the general public on death penalty by inviting learned and reputed persons to speak on this subject matter, holding film festivals on the topic of capital punishment and training journalists on how to impart education about the death penalty to the public (Blok & Suter, 2017). Human rights organizations in Zimbabwe have gone a step further by writing open letters to leading political parties of the country, putting up billboards and organizing processions to put pressure and create an impact on society in order to gather support for the abolition of death penalty (Zilala, 2013).

4.4 Role of Media in Shaping Public Opinion

There are only a handful of people in any given country that have a direct interaction with the criminal justice system. The rest of the population internalizes its notions about the system through what they see from media coverage (Bandes, 2004). Here lies our biggest problem in affording public opinion polls such a heavy weightage in the creation, enforcement, and implementation of laws around the issue of death penalty. The ways in which the media depicts and displays real-life events can completely mold and distort the public opinion on a given issue in several different ways (Jha, 2015). The most recent examples of this are the Sheena Bohra murder case (2012), the Salman Khan hit-and-run case (2002), and the Aarushi Talwar murder case (2008). In all of these cases, before the court even passed its verdict, the entire nation was convinced that the accused were guilty based on what the media had displayed. This negates the fundamental truth of justice that goes by the saying "*innocent until proven guilty*" which has also been codified under Article 11 of The Universal Declaration of Human Rights (UDHR). The UDHR is a document adopted by the United Nations General Assembly, which lays down the obligations of the international community to respect the rights and freedom to which every human being is entitled.

Capital crimes such as murder, rape, terrorism, etc. tend to be "newsworthy" for the media as they easily catch the attention of readers/viewers. The media does not simply present these events as they occur in society. Their coverage is suited to "marketing and economic" strategies that will help them sell their story. Nearly 81% of Americans said that they judged the intensity of a crime based on what they saw on the media rather than from personal experience (Beale, 2006). In another poll, people were asked to identify where they received their information about the criminal justice system of which 41% identified television news channels, 37% identified news magazines, and 36% identified newspapers (American Bar Association Poll, 1999).

The media employs two tactics while delivering information to the public. The first is "agenda-setting" which is directed at diverting the public attention to particular issues. The second is "priming effects" which is directed at affecting the criteria by which viewers judge public policies and public officials (Beale, 2006). This shows the media's ability to cause the public to perceive crime in a more alarming and perilous manner than it actually appears to be. These are particularly manipulative when one does not have a personal experience with respect to a particular issue (Pearse, 2001).

Furthermore, depiction of crimes in a gory manner not only grabs the public attention easily but also affects the public confidence in the criminal justice system in the event when the offender is set free. The O.J. Simpson trial wherein the offender was accused of the murder of his wife Nicole Simpson and her friend Ron Goldman was so heavily publicized by the media that the people of the nation lost faith in the judicial system when he was acquitted of both the murders (Beale, 2006). In the Nirbhaya Rape Case, the Juvenile Justice Bill was amended in 2015 to change the age of an adult from 18 years to 16 years. This was done due to a juvenile being one of the accused in the case. This case was followed closely and publicized on every aspect by the media for a long period of time. The media revealed that the juvenile was the one who lured Nirbhaya and her friend into entering the bus, committed acts of rape on her, and inserted a rod into her body. However, he was sent to a juvenile justice home and released after 3 years. He now works as a chef in South India and is roaming free (Maanvi, 2017). Such instances make the public lose faith in the judiciary and a large part of this feeling of hopelessness stems from the limited knowledge about the crime that the media makes available to the public. This lack of confidence, in turn, sparks vehemence and feelings of resentment with the need for a more secure environment thereby leading to the formation of a belief that death penalty, due to its harsh nature and consequence, is the solution to such atrocities.

4.5 Conclusion

While it is important to form a concise questionnaire/survey covering all the important aspects as discussed above to help us gage accurate representations for public support of death penalty, the public opinion will not be conclusive in any given situation as there are always some loopholes such as lack of awareness and bias which can further be distorted by the media. Public opinion based on such discrepancies can hold no value. Before judges and legislators use public opinion in judicial decision-making and drafting legislations, respectively, these defects must be removed to get an accurate representation of what the public really wants. While lack of awareness and distortion of thought by the media can be cured by making sure the public is well informed of all the factors essential in coming to its decision, it is the problem of bias which simply cannot be eliminated from the system as a whole. Bias is inherent in any given society. It is impossible to segregate the Black from the White, the rich from the poor, or the highly qualified from the less educated as they all co-exist in society.

As early as 1971, John Rawls proposed in his Theory of Justice a utopian solution to the notion of inherent bias. Rawls believed that if all the people in society were at an equally footing right from the start, then any principle that they agreed upon for the governance of their society would be fair (Rawls, 1971). For example, if everyone in a particular country was born white with an equal amount of skill, talent, and wealth, any governing principles which they agreed upon (e.g., democratic, communist, socialist state, etc.) would be fair. He called this an original position of equality.

In order to legitimize the original position of equality, he came up with the concept of the "veil of ignorance." The veil of ignorance deprives people of all "knowledge of their personal characteristics and historical circumstances" (Freeman, 2016). To put it simply, people are not aware of whether they are rich or poor, black or white, male or female, young or old, etc. They do not know anything about themselves. The parties in this original position under the veil of ignorance are "presented with a list of the main conceptions of justice drawn from the tradition of social and political philosophy, and are assigned the task of choosing from among these alternatives the conception of justice that best advances their interests" (*ibid.*). This concept seems bizarre and merely idealistic; distant from reality as it begs the question: What would be each individual's stance on capital punishment be if they did not know their sex, race, income level, educational qualifications, age, etc. and what are the reasons for them coming to these decisions at this "original position of equality"? This theory, while extremely powerful, cannot be applied in any modern society as it is utopian and far-fetched. Bias can never be eliminated 100%. The problem of bias is what makes the public opinion unreliable. The common man will always be guided by this inherent bias and his emotions while taking any decision.

In most countries, neither the approval nor the removal of a judge is a task delegated to the public. However, judges are still guided by public opinion for two primary reasons. The first is when a judge has been nominated but his appointment is still pending. In such a situation, if the public opinion is in favor of the death penalty, "it is highly implausible that a candidate who refused to take a strong position in favor of the death penalty would be elected" (Bandes, 2004). The second is subsequent to the appointment of the judge. In such a situation, judges may be concerned with upholding what can be termed as "institutional legitimacy" which we have analyzed through case laws wherein the judiciary has examined the public opinion prior to reaching its verdict (Voeten, 2013). However, it would be incorrect to judge the public opinion based on the limitations of bias as discussed above as it is the life of a man that is in question. The legislature, executive, and judiciary have to be free from bias for justice to be served. Since bias can never be eliminated wholly, it is pertinent to ask whether public opinion must be taken in deciding the fate of a man, and how much weight, if any, must be attached to this public opinion or whether the issue should be decided on the basis of a fundamental principle of human rights, and not of opinion?

References

American Bar Association Poll of the Criminal Justice System. (1999). Retrieved from http://www.abanet.org/media/perception/perceptions.pdf.

Applegate, B. K., J. P. Wright, R. G. Dunaway, F. T. Cullen, and J. D. Wooldredge. (1993). Victim-offender race and support for capital punishment: A factorial design approach. *American Journal of Criminal Justice, 18*(1), 95–115.

Australian Human Rights Commission. United Nations Association of Australia. (2006). *The death penalty—A matter of principle*. Retrieved from https://www.humanrights.gov.au/news/speeches/death-penalty-matter-principle#endnote1.

Bandes, S. (2004). Fear factor: The role of media in covering and shaping the death penalty. *Ohio State Journal of Criminal Law, 1*, 585–597.

Barkan, S., & Cohn, S. (2005). Why whites favor spending more money to fight crime: The role of racial prejudice. *Social Problems, 52*(2), 300–314.

Beale, S. (2006). The news media's influence on criminal justice policy: How market driven news promotes punitiveness. *William and Mary Law Review, 48*, 397–481.

Blok, Z., & Suter C. (2017). *Triggers for abolition of the death penalty in Africa: A Southern African perspective* (pp. 10–32). International Federation on Human Rights, The Botswana Centre for Human Rights.

Chenwi, L. (2005). *Towards the abolition of the death penalty in Africa: A human rights perspective* (pp. 120–140). University of Pretoria.

Choudhri, S., & Hiremath, V. (n.d.). Public opinion on death penalty: An emperical study in Belagavi City, Karnataka India. *International Journal of Social Legal Analysis and Rural Development, 3*(2), 48–52.

Cornell Centre on Death Penalty Worldwide. (2014). *Death penalty database*. Cornell Law School. Retrieved from http://www.deathpenaltyworldwide.org/country-search-post.cfm?country=united+states+of+america.

Dugger, A. (n.d.). *What is public opinion?* Retrieved from https://study.com/academy/lesson/what-is-public-opinion.html.

Ellsworth, P. C., & Ross, L. (1983). Public opinion and capital punishment: A close examination of the views of abolitionists and retentionists. *Crime and Delinquency, 29*, 120–169.

Foucault, M. (1975). *Discipline and punish: The birth of the prison* (pp. 3–20). New York: Pantheon Books.

Freeman, S. (2016). *Original position*. Stanford Encyclopedia of Philosophy (Winter 2016 Edition). Retrieved from https://plato.stanford.edu/entries/original-position/.

Gallup Poll. (2017). *Death penalty*. Retrieved from http://news.gallup.com/poll/1606/death-penalty.aspx.

Goodsir, D. (2003). *Tracing a killer smile*. The Age. Retrieved from https://www.theage.com.au/articles/2003/08/05/1059849389919.html.

Hood, R. (2013). *The death penalty in Malaysia: Public opinion on the mandatory death penalty for drug trafficking murder and firearms offences*. Centre for Criminology. University of Oxford. London: The Death Penalty Project, pp. 1–41.

Hood, R & Seemungal, F. (2011). *Public opinion on the mandatory death penalty in Trinidad*. A Report for the Death Penalty Project and the Rights Advocacy Project of the University of the West Indies Faculty of Law, pp. 1–5.

Human Sciences Research Council. (1996). Rights or Wrongs: Public Attitudes Towards Moral Values. *HSRC Review*, *2*(3), 4–5. Retrieved from http://www.hsrc.ac.za/uploads/pageContent/1607/Rights%20or%20Wrongs.pdf.

Hummer, L. (2014). *I witnessed Ohio's execution of Dennis McGuire: What I saw was inhumane.* The Guardian. Retrieved from https://www.theguardian.com/commentisfree/2014/jan/22/ohio-mcguire-execution-untested-lethal-injection-inhumane.

United Nations. Convention against Torture and Other Cruel, Inhuman or Degrading Treatment or Punishment. (2014). Retrieved from https://legal.un.org/avl/pdf/ha/catcidtp/catcidtp_e.pdf.

Jha, N. (2015). *Constitutionality of media trials: A detailed analysis.* Academike. Retrieved from https://www.lawctopus.com/academike/media-trials-india/.

Jha, J. (2017). *The death penalty in South Asia.* The Diplomat. Retrieved from https://thediplomat.com/2017/05/the-death-penalty-in-south-asia/.

Kelley, J., & Braithwaite, J. (1990). Public opinion and the death penalty in Australia. *Justice Quarterly, Academy of Criminal Justice Sciences, 7*(3), 538–553.

Kentish, B. (2017). *Half of leave voters want to bring back the death penalty after Brexit.* Independent. Retrieved from https://www.independent.co.uk/news/uk/politics/brexit-poll-leave-voters-death-penalty-yougov-results-light-bulbs-a7656791.html.

Lane, J. (2015). Capital punishment: *Where and why it's practiced in Asia.* Asian Correspondent. Retrieved from https://asiancorrespondent.com/2015/04/capital-punishment-where-and-why-its-practiced-in-asia/#E5oTe6q4XQ2ZR3PE.97.

Live Law Research Team. (2016). *Public opinion towards death penalty.* Live Law. Retrieved from http://www.livelaw.in/public-opinion-towards-death-penalty/.

Maanvi. (2017). *Where's the Juvenile in the Nirbhaya Case? A Cook at a Dhaba & Unaware.* The Quint. Retrieved from https://www.thequint.com/voices/fighting-rape/four-yrs-post-nirbhaya-juvenile-accused-is-a-cook-at-a-dhaba-december-2012-jyoti-singh-damini-sexual-assault-gang.

Mana. (2016). *The amazing escape from hangman's noose.* The Times Group. Retrieved from http://www.times.mw/the-amazing-escape-from-hangmans-noose/.

Markowitz, M., & Harver, W. (2003). Public sentiment on the death penalty: Do race, gender, age, & state of mind matter? *National Social Science Journal, 21*(1).

Midgley, J. (1974). Pubic opinion and the death penalty in South Africa. *The British Journal of Criminology, 14*(4), 345–358.

Muir, C. (2017). *Goodbye, my darlings'-remembering the trauma of Australia's last execution.* The Guardian. Retrieved from https://www.theguardian.com/world/2017/feb/04/goodbye-my-darlings-remembering-the-trauma-of-australias-last-execution.

N.A. (2006). *PM happy over death penalty stance.* The Age. Retrieved from https://www.theage.com.au/news/National/PM-happy-over-death-penalty-stance/2006/09/15/1157827138953.html.

N.A. (2013). *Crime and punishment. Public perception, judgment and opinion.* Penal Reform International. Satio Group of Companies, Department of Sociological and Marketing Research. Retrieved from https://s16889.pcdn.co/wp-content/uploads/2014/02/Belarus-public-opinion-survey-English-for-publication1.pdf.

N.A. (2015). *India's history of capital punishment in the last decade.* India Today. Retrieved from https://www.indiatoday.in/education-today/gk-current-affairs/story/indias-history-of-capital-punishment-in-the-last-decade-285526-2015-07-30.

N.A. (2017a). *Death penalty fast facts.* CNN Library. Retrieved from https://edition.cnn.com/2013/07/19/us/death-penalty-fast-facts/index.html.

N.A. (2017b). *Death penalties in Asia.* The Nation. Retrieved from http://www.nationmultimedia.com/detail/aec/30313732.

N.A. (2017c). *EU local statement on abolition of the death penalty.* Delegation of the European Union to the Council of Europe. Retrieved from https://eeas.europa.eu/delegations/council-europe/34161/eu-local-statement-abolition-death-penalty_en.

N.A. (n.d.) *Death Penalty Information Centre. International polls and studies.* Retrieved from https://deathpenaltyinfo.org/international-polls-and-studies.

N.A. (n.d.). *Death Penalty Information Centre. United Kingdom Marks 50th Anniversary of Death Penalty Abolition.* Retrieved from https://deathpenaltyinfo.org/node/6296.

Pearse, E. & (2001). *Media effects and society* (pp. 200–320). Taylor and Francis Group, New York.

Rawls, J. (1971). *A theory of justice* (pp. 632–643). Cambridge, MA: Belknap Press of Harvard University Press.

Sato, M. (2014). *The death penalty in Japan: Will the public tolerate abolition?* (pp. 37–46). UK: Springer.

Smith, O. (2018). *Mapped: The 53 places that still have the death penalty-including Japan.* The Telegraph. Retrieved from https://www.telegraph.co.uk/travel/maps-and-graphics/countries-that-still-have-the-death-penalty/.

Stern, J. (2015). *The cruel and unusual execution of clayton lockett.* The Atlantic. Retrieved from https://www.theatlantic.com/magazine/archive/2015/06/execution-clayton-lockett/392069/.

Strange, C. (2018). *The anniversary of Steven Truscott's death sentence: From guilt to innocence.* The Conversation. Retrieved from http://theconversation.com/the-anniversary-of-steven-truscotts-death-sentence-from-guilt-to-innocence-103671.

Study on the Question of the Death Penalty in Africa, Submitted by the Working Group on the Death Penalty in Africa in accordance with Resolution ACHPR/Res.79 (XXXVIII) 05, Adopted by The African Commission on Human and Peoples' Rights at its 50th Ordinary Session (24 October–07 November 2011) Banjul, The Gambia.

Tagusari, M. (2010). Death penalty in Japan. *East Asian Law Journal, 1* (2), 93–106.

Tankebe, J., & Boakye, K. (2016). *A pioneering study of public opinion on death penalty in Ghana suggests unpopularity of the death penalty as punishment for crime.* Death Penalty Worldwide. Cornell Law School. Retrieved from http://blog.deathpenaltyworldwide.org/2016/02/a-pioneering-study-of-public-opinion-on-the-death-penalty-in-ghana-suggests-the-unpopularity-of-the-.html.

Tankebe, J., Boakye, K., & Atupare, A. (2015). Public opinion on the death penalty in Ghana. *Centre for Criminology and Criminal Justice,* 35–40.

Tyler, T., & Weber, R. (1982). Support for the death penalty; instrumental response to crime or symbolic attitude? *Law and Society Review, 17*(1), 21–46.

Unnever, J., & Cullen, F. (2005). Executing the innocent and support for capital punishment: Implications for public policy. *Criminology and Public Policy, 4*(1), 3–37.

Vidmar, N., & Ellsworth, P. (1974). Public opinion on death penalty. *Stanford Law Review, 26,* 1245–1255.

Vito, G. F., & Keil, T. J. (1998). Elements of support for the capital punishment: An examination of changing attitudes. *Journal of Crime and Justice, 21*(2), 17–36.

Voeten, E. (2013). *How the Supreme Court responds to public opinion.* Washington Monthly. Retrieved from https://washingtonmonthly.com/2013/06/28/how-the-supreme-court-responds-to-public-opinion/.

Vollum, S., & Buffington-Vollum, J. (2010). An examination of social-psychological factors and support for the death penalty: Attribution, moral disengagement, and the value-expressive function of attitudes. *American Journal of Criminal Justice, 35*(1–2), 15–36.

York, B. (2017). *Capital punishment in Australia.* National Library of Australia. Retrieved from https://www.nla.gov.au/unbound/capital-punishment-in-australia.

YouGov Survey. (2015). *Poll results: Death penalty.* Retrieved from https://today.yougov.com/news/2015/07/07/poll-results-death-penalty/.

Zhang, L. (2014). *China's death penalty debate.* The New York Times. Retrieved from https://www.nytimes.com/2014/12/30/opinion/chinas-death-penalty-debate.html.

Zilala, C. (2013). *A big step closer to abolishing the death penalty in Zimbabwe.* Amnesty International. Retrieved from https://www.amnesty.org/en/latest/campaigns/2013/11/a-big-step-closer-to-abolishing-the-death-penalty-in-zimbabwe/.

Zimring, F., & Johnson, D. (2012). Public opinion and death penalty reform in the People's Republic of China. *City University of Hong Kong Law Review, 3*(2), 189–196.

Zitrin, E. (2015) *The African continent on the road to the abolition of death penalty.* Retrieved from http://www.fiacat.org/opinion-piece-the-african-continent-on-the-road-to-the-abolition-of-the-death-penalty.

Zlotnick, M. (1996). The death penalty and the public opinion. *South African Journal on Human Rights*, 70–79.

Chapter 5
Psychosocial Factors Associated with Death Penalty: *Impact on Families of Victims, Families of Defendants and the "Others"*

5.1 Introduction

The extant literature on death penalty is mostly focused upon arguments in favor or in opposition to death penalty as a punishment for heinous crimes such as murder (e.g., Hood & Hoyle, 2009; Nicolau, 2013; Radelet & Borg, 2000; Zhigang, 2009). Arguments in this area generally revolve around the human rights perspective and deterrence effect of death penalty (Amnesty International, 2007; Lacock & Radelet, 2009; Radelet & Borg, 2000; United Nations Human Rights Council, 2012). Several public opinion polls on death penalty have been conducted in various parts of the world to understand the public perception about death sentence and have provided mixed results that vary according to factors like nature of the crime (Death Penalty Information Center, 2015). However, the perspectives of family members and those closely involved in the execution process need to be explored in more detail (Mitchell, 2013). In the context of state executions, previous research studies used the term "secondary trauma" (Adcock, 2010; Gil, Johnson, & Johnson, 2006; Seemungal, Seal, & Black, 2016) to refer to the "distress, harm, and injuries suffered by individuals other than the condemned prisoner" (Gil et al., 2006, p. 371). Crime victims' families experience grief due to victimization of their loved one (Beck, Blackwell, Leonard, & Mears, 2002; King, 2004), feelings of retribution (Burns, 2006; King, 2006; Radelet & Borg, 2000), engage in self-blame (Asaro, 2001), face financial burden, increased risk for mental disorders (Amick-McMullan, Kilpatrick, & Resnick, 1991; Asaro, 2001; Zinzow, Rheingold, Hawkins, Saunders, & Kilpatrick, 2009), pressure to act according to the ideal scheme of a victim's family (Berns, 2009; King, 2006), stressful court proceedings (Armour, 2002; Burns, 2006; King, 2003, 2004), distress due to media "trials" (Armour, 2002; Bandes, 2000; Goodwin, 1997) and the need to attain closure (Armour, 2002; Asaro, 2001; Sharp, 2005). Families of defendants report similar yet distinct experiences including initial shock (Beck et al., 2002; Sharp, 2005), anticipatory and disenfranchised grief (Doka, 1989; Jones & Beck, 2007; Sharp, 2005; Vandiver, 1998), financial burden (Beck et al., 2002; Sharp, 2005), negative media attention (Eschholz, Reed, Beck, & Leonard, 2003),

S. P. Sahni and M. Junnarkar, *The Death Penalty*,
https://doi.org/10.1007/978-981-15-3129-3_5

increased risk for mental disorders (Beck et al., 2002; Eschholz et al., 2003; King & Norgard, 1999; Sharp, 2016), distressful court proceedings, isolation, and stigma (Beck et al., 2002; King, 2004; King & Norgard, 1999; Sharp, 2005). Apart from the families of defendants and victims, others who interact with the defendant such as lawyers, executioners, and prison guards are also negatively affected. These professionals have reported moral disengagement with their work (Osofsky, Bandura, & Zimbardo, 2005) and Post-Traumatic Stress Disorder (PTSD) like symptoms such as nightmares, sleep disturbances, and loss of appetite (Adcock, 2010; Antonio, 2006, 2008; Bienen, 1992; DeLilly, 2014; Gil et al., 2006; Lifton & Mitchell, 2000; Penal Reform International, 2014, 2015a, b; Seemungal et al., 2016; Slick, 2011).

To shed light onto this area, this chapter presents a review of literature on the wide range of perceptions and psychosocial impact of death sentence on the families of victims, families of the defendants, and other groups who interact with a capital defendant. These individuals are directly affected by the death sentence and thus special focus needs to be directed toward understanding their perspectives. The chapter is divided into three sections. The first section discusses the impact of death sentence on a victim's family using past research and theoretical conceptualizations. The second section presents an overview of the research conducted to understand the effect of capital punishment on the family of a defendant. In the third section, the authors discuss the impact of being involved in the capital punishment process on individuals such as lawyers, jurors, prison staff, execution teams, and execution witnesses. Lastly, the authors conclude the chapter by presenting a short note on the limitations of past research and the need for further future studies in this area.

5.2 Experience of Victims' Families in Death Penalty Cases

An unnatural death of a family member due to homicide is far more difficult to cope with than a death under natural circumstances (King, 2004). Family members of the victim experience helplessness and have repeated thoughts about how their loved one was victimized (Armour, 2002; Asaro, 2001). Self-blame and guilt for not being able to protect the victim is prominent and thus coping with the death is problematic for the family (Asaro, 2001). The untimely death also places several unanticipated demands upon the family such as identification of victim's body, engaging with the criminal justice system, paying medical bills, and loss of victim's income (Asaro, 2001; King, 2004). Furthermore, empirical evidence has documented distress and frustration among victims' families toward the criminal justice system (Armour, 2002; Burns, 2006; King, 2003, 2004). Some families perceive disappointment as they are unable to play an active part in the court's proceedings and decisions. Alongside, media coverage of the victim is seen to act as a deterrent in coping with the traumatic incident (Goodwin, 1997). A victim's family thus deals with the criminal justice system and also encounters an active public and media trial (Armour, 2002; Bandes, 2000).

5.2.1 *Theoretical Models Used to Explain Experiences of Victims' Families in Death Penalty Cases*

Some theoretical models that are commonly used by researchers to study the experiences of a victim's family are grief theory, PTSD, and the concept of closure. The following section discusses each of these three models.

5.2.1.1 Post-Traumatic Stress Disorder (PTSD)

Empirical studies have documented an increased vulnerability of murder victims' families towards mental disorders like PTSD, depression, anxiety disorders, and substance abuse (Amick-McMullan et al., 1991; Asoro, 2001; Zinzow et al., 2009). Post-Traumatic Stress Disorder (PTSD) is a type of mental disorder that is triggered after a traumatic event. According to the Diagnostic and Statistical Manual of Mental Disorder–5 (DSM 5) (American Psychiatric Association, 2013), PTSD can be triggered even in cases wherein individuals learn that a traumatic event occurred to a person closely known to them. To explain the occurrence and maintenance of PTSD symptoms among family survivors of homicide victims, Amick-McMullan, Kilpatrick, Veronen, and Smith (1989) utilized the model of Mowrer's Two Factor Learning Theory. In this model, factor one is classical conditioning. This factor suggests that when a previously neutral stimulus (like a news channel, telephone ring, etc.) is paired with the traumatic disclosure of a family member's murder, then the latter encounters with the neutral stimuli alone are followed by emotional and cognitive disturbances which are usually experienced after a traumatic event. The second factor in this model is stimulus generalization, which suggests that gradually various stimuli similar to the initially neutral stimuli lead to responses that are usually evoked after a traumatic event. This model offers one explanation of how interaction with the criminal justice system and the repeated presentation of traumatic information to the family members of the victim can increase their risk toward experiencing PTSD like symptoms (Amick-McMullan et al., 1989).

5.2.1.2 Grief Theory

Grief is the natural response to a symbolic or tangible loss of something valued by an individual (Rainer, 2013). According to Kübler-Ross (1969), individuals facing the loss of a loved one, go through the stages of denial, anger, bargaining, depression, and acceptance. Although every person may not go through each of these stages in a prescribed order, yet, the stage theory provides a broad model to understand the process of grief (Kübler-Ross, 1969). In the specific case of a victim's family, the shock of the murder and the resultant trauma complicate the normal grieving process (Beck et al., 2002; King, 2004). Factors such as media coverage of the crime can prolong a victim's family's bereavement (Goodwin, 1997). Constant media attention hampers the scope to "privately" mourn the loss of the victim and the mourning instead becomes a "public" experience (Armour, 2002; Bandes, 2000). In addition, interaction with the criminal justice system and involvement in lengthy death penalty trials, serve to lengthen the grieving process and lead to protracted grief (Adcock, 2010).

5.2.1.3 Victim's Family and Closure

The initial reactions of the victims' family are followed by attempts to work through their grief and seek some sort of closure. Closure involves a "recursive series of adjustments" (Madeira, 2010, p. 1481) that involves a "constellation of feelings—peace, relief, a sense of justice, the ability to move on—that comes with finality" (Bandes, 2009, p. 3). There is no one way in which families experience closure—for some, closure is achieved through forgiveness or interactions with the perpetrator to get details regarding the victims' death; for others, closure may mean punishment for the perpetrator (Berns, 2009).

The impact of death penalty on a victim's family and their response toward this experience varies based on the category they belong to (Adcock, 2010), viz.

(a) Those who do not support death penalty;
(b) Those who support death penalty but, in whose case, the court did not give a death sentence to the perpetrator;
(c) Those who support death penalty and the court granted death penalty to the perpetrator.

Feelings of retribution and severe punishment for the accused are not uncommon among victim's families belonging to the second and third groups. Many follow the eye for an eye dictum and want the accused to get a death sentence. Burns (2006), through a qualitative study, demonstrated that family members of victims were unable to forgive the offender and believed that the impending death penalty was justified. Researchers (Radelet & Borg, 2000; King, 2006; Adcock, 2010) have noted that victims' families place the value of their loved one upon the severity of punishment given to the accused. Death penalty creates a hierarchy of victims wherein the perpetrators of only those who were severely violated get a death sentence. Therefore, when death penalty is not granted, some family members experience frustration due to the "lesser" value accorded to the life of their loved one and form the perception that life of their family member was not "worth the life of a killer" (Radelet & Borg, 2000, p. 53).

Contrastingly, some victims' families do not support and rather strongly oppose death penalty as a punishment for the accused. Victim family groups such as "Murder Victims Families for Reconciliation" and movements such as "Declaration to Life" have actively advocated to abolish death penalty (Logan, 1999). However, such families face significant challenges in making their opinion public. "Good" victims' families (King, 2006) are expected to act in a manner that is indicative of their support for the severest punishment. Therefore, families face discrimination

(Sharp, 2005) if they have an opinion contrary to these institutionalized sets of "feeling rules" (Berns, 2009, p. 384). In the book, *Don't Kill in Our Names: Families of Murder Victims Speak Out Against the Death Penalty* King (2003), presented an analysis based on the interviews with victims' families that opposed the death penalty. King (2003) highlighted that voices of victims' families are silenced and that adopting a stance contrary to death penalty is questioned by the criminal justice system and the society in general. Family members may have several reasons for not supporting death penalty. One reason provided by a victim's mother in King's (2003) research was that she didn't "want to memorialize the life of her beautiful, loving daughter by killing a sick human being" (King, 2006, p. 295). At other times, family members view the lengthy trial period as a deterrent in seeking death penalty (Bandes, 2000; Radelet & Borg, 2000). Furthermore, within the family of the victim itself, members may take opposing stances toward death penalty which contributes to strain in existing relationships (King, 2006).

On the other hand, many scholars suggest that "closure is for doors" (Chinni & Grier, 2001) and neither death penalty nor forgiveness (Adcock, 2010; Madeira, 2010) leads to complete closure. On similar lines, Madeira (2010) stated that closure is a process rather than an outcome. Usage of the "closure argument" as a support for death penalty in court as a part of therapeutic jurisprudence has been criticized by scholars citing the false hope it generates among victims' families attempting to attain closure (Adcock, 2010; Bandes, 2009; Berns, 2009; Madeira, 2010). Madeira (2010) postulated that the "closure claim" is politicized. She proposed that rather than being therapeutic, the hope for closure puts at stake the emotions of a victim's family and contributes to further trauma. Overall, there is a paucity of conclusive empirical support for death penalty as a means to attain closure. For instance, Eaton and Christensen (2014) through a mixed methods study examined the statements of co-victims after an offender's execution. Their study demonstrated that co-victims were divided regarding whether execution provided them closure. More importantly, it was observed that the negative correlation of death penalty with feelings of revenge gradually grew insignificant with time (Eaton & Christensen, 2014).

5.3 Experience of Capital Defendants' Families

Family members of the defendant face distress at various stages of the death penalty judgement. They face stressors such as knowledge of the crime that their family member is accused of, court trials, notification of the death sentence, media, community, prison visits, and lastly the execution (Beck et al., 2002). The defendant's family experiences an initial shock after being intimated about the criminal act and arrest, followed by an uncertainty regarding the future of their loved one and their family (Sharp, 2005). The experience of court trials is equally disturbing (King, 2004; Sharp, 2005). The situation of those relatives wherein the victim and accused come from the same families is even worse; in the words of Sharp (2005, p. 131), they are "double losers." Researchers have documented that the defendant's family may perceive the criminal justice system to be unjust and biased toward the victim's family (Beck et al., 2002; King, 2004). A participant in Beck et al. (2002) reported that, "you know you are not as good as the victim's side—they get water and you get nothing." Ostracization in their neighborhood, workplace, school, etc., also contributes to the overall stigma and stress faced by the family members (Beck et al., 2002; King, 2004; Sharp, 2005). Families are pacified by the option of visiting and meeting their loved one; however, prison visits serve as another reminder of the impending death of their family member. At times, the treatment and condition of prisoners in jails can negatively affect the coping mechanisms of the family (Beck et al., 2002). Several cases of death penalty are covered extensively by media. The media often portrays a skewed image of the accused and excessively sensationalizes the events which contributes to frustration and stigmatization of the entire family. Tendency of the media to present news using the common narrative of "good against evil" consequently leaves the defendant's side of the story unexplored (Eschholz et al., 2003, p. 20).

The detrimental impact of death penalty on children of death row prisoners is another issue of concern. Lack of information about the execution, helplessness due to inability to protect parent through participation in trials, restricted prison visitation, and grief of losing an attachment figure severely impacts children and increases their vulnerability toward other problems (Robertson & Brett, 2013; Ssuubi, 2016). Children of death row prisoners are at a higher risk for substance abuse, truancy, violence, and mental health problems such as PTSD (Ssuubi, 2016). In 2013, the United Nations Human Rights Council (UNHRC) recognized this negative impact and adopted "Resolution 22/11." In accordance with the Convention on Rights of the Child, this resolution called for action from governments to extend support for children whose parents are sentenced to death. It also urged for assistance in the form of providing children with information and access to their parents (UNHRC, 2013).

5.3.1 Comparison of Experiences of Victim's and Defendant's Family: Grief Theory

From the above discussion, it follows that the experiences of the victim's and offender's families are quite comparable (Beck et al., 2002; King, 2004; Sharp, 2005). Like the victim's family, the offender's family also faces trauma and grief due to loss of a family member. Depression (Beck et al., 2002; Eschholz et al., 2003; King & Norgard, 1999; Sharp, 2016), PTSD, and anxiety (Eschholz et al., 2003; Sharp, 2016) were found to be prevalent among the offender's family members. Similar to a victim's family members, an accused's family also faces financial problems. The accused may be a source of income for the family, therefore an arrest would mean loss of the family's income. In addition, the legal process may be another reason for further expenditure (Beck et al., 2002; Sharp, 2005).

In many ways, however, the impact of a death sentence on the offender's family is distinct. The grief experienced by an accused's family is significantly different since "true" loss (death) has not occurred. The defendant's family faces "anticipatory grief," i.e., grief in anticipation of losing their loved one to execution (Vandiver, 1998). Another characteristic of the grief of a defendant's family is that unlike a victim's family their concerns are invalidated by the society (Doka, 1989; Jones & Beck, 2007). Researchers Jones and Beck (2007) examined this concept of "disenfranchised grief" through interviews of 26 families of death row inmates. The results indicated that the society saw no need for grief after the execution of a "criminal" and thus, did not validate the sorrow of these family members. In addition, grief of defendants' families is also "protracted" since death of a loved one is impending, and a continuous sense of loss is experienced till the final execution (Sharp, 2016). Therefore, several models have been used to define the impact of death penalty on a death row inmate's family; however, each of these theoretical concepts describes only some aspects of the reactions of this group. Overall, the impact of death penalty on families of defendants is complex and varied (Jones & Beck, 2007). Sharp (2005) elaborated on this complex nature of grief and used Kübler-Ross's (1969) stages of grief to explain the repetitive BADD (bargaining, activity, disillusionment, desperation) cycle of grief that family members of defendants go through. At first, family members oscillate between denial and shock in response to the criminal act of the loved one. Thereafter, the family members experience hope, despair, and disillusionment as they bargain with higher authorities and the criminal justice system. Subsequently, families begin to accept death sentence as the reality and lastly, adjust to the news of the execution or the final decision of the court. Families may progress through these common stages in a linear or non-linear manner (Sharp, 2016). Apart from the distinct type of grief experienced, another significant difference between the victim's and defendant's family is the support they receive that subsequently aids their coping process. Support groups and assistance that the defendants' families receive from the government is limited (King & Norgard, 1999; Sharp, 2005). Due to the lack of support, the defendants' families often feel that even they are sentenced along with the accused (Sharp, 2005). Some community members believe that an accused's family's suffering is a natural consequence of the accused's deeds, thus the society has no role to play in supporting them, rather, the limited resources should be directed toward an innocent victim's family (King, 2004).

5.4 Experiences of "Others" in Death Penalty Cases

There is limited research on the social impact of the death penalty on people other than the victim's and defendant's families (Gil et al., 2006). These "others" involved in the death penalty cases include prison staff (wardens, guards), executioners, strap-down team, death row lawyers, jurors, spiritual advisors, medical and mental health practitioners, witnesses to an execution and journalists[1] (Adcock, 2010; Gil et al., 2006; Osofsky & Osofsky, 2002). The extant research articles on this population mostly draw from limited systematic research, retrospective accounts, anecdotes, and memoirs (Gil et al., 2006). This is despite these professionals being closely engaged in the execution process. The following sections discuss the impact of death sentence on (a) lawyers and jurors involved in handling these cases, (b) prison staff present in the jail where the death row inmate is imprisoned and the execution team that conducts the prisoner's execution, and lastly (c) the individuals who present themselves as witnesses to the final execution.

5.4.1 Experiences of Jurors and Lawyers

Jurors who serve in capital trials experience the pressure of being the decider of life or death for the defendant (Antonio, 2006, 2008; Bienen, 1992). Research indicates that the impact of a capital trial on jurors can be observed both during and after the trial has ended (Antonio, 2006, 2008). While the trial is under progress, jurors listen and view graphic details of the crime which may be disturbing. In addition, defence and prosecution lawyers may try to portray the defendant/victim in an emotional light by highlighting their humaneness and human relationships that the victim/defendant share with their family members to build the case for their client (Antonio, 2008). Jurors also experience frustration due to the responsibility to make a decision that would inevitably leave one of the parties dissatisfied (Antonio, 2006). As part of a qualitative study conducted by Bienen (1992), one of the jurors metaphorically compared the challenge of decision-making in capital trials to the Vietnam war. He conveyed the pressure he experienced and reported (Bienen, 1992, p. 1347).

> I think that's the most pressure – Vietnam was a piece of cake compared to that. When you're sitting there and you know that you're holding a man's life – you know it's one thing to be in a combat situation and know that that's the enemy. But to sit there and look at another human being and know that you and eleven other people have the responsibility of life and death.

Once the trial has ended some jurors experience lingering effects of the trial and in some cases long-term effects are also observed. In retrospect, some jurors may consider their experience at a capital trial as "rewarding and educational," while some may also report comparatively less positive experiences (Antonio, 2006). Research (Antonio, 2006; Bienen, 1992) has shown that some jurors felt emotionally drained after a capital trial, had persistent thoughts about the trial and fear of being harmed by the victim/defendant. Other studies refer to such experiences as post-jury blues, which include nightmares, sleep disturbances, and loss of appetite (Antonio, 2006; Bienen, 1992). Antonio (2008) further explored the various facets of jurors' experience of capital trials as part of a larger research initiative called the Capital Jury

[1] This list will vary from one country to another based on the country's laws and procedures in place for death penalty inmates.

Project (USA).[2] The findings of this study indicated that over 60% of the respondents found the process of serving on the capital trial as "emotionally upsetting," and 36% reported troubles in sleeping and eating during or after the trial. Gender differences in the responses were also observed since more females than male jurors reported sleeping/appetite problems (M = 47.7%, F = 23.7%) and feeling emotionally upset (M = 70.8%, F = 50.4%) during/after the trial (Antonio, 2008).

Like jurors, lawyers also experience significant stress during capital trials. The UN Secretary-General's 2015 report to the Human Rights Council on the death penalty, recognized the potential negative impact of execution on lawyers and strongly put forth the need to address the issue of mental health of death row lawyers and aid their families as well (Penal Reform International, 2015a). It has been reported that criminal defence lawyers may not be well equipped to handle the emotional consequences of a capital trial (Adcock, 2010). High stakes of the trial (i.e., life or death of the client) place lawyers in a stressful situation (Seemungal et al., 2016). Some lawyers have reported experiencing vicarious trauma and an ongoing cycle of hope and despair during the trial (Adcock, 2010). Seemungal et al. (2016) presented anecdotes of some lawyers who were verbally abused and received threats via telephone calls. A lawyer from India has described his personal experience as follows (Penal Reform International, 2014, p. 2):

> I specialize in end-stage death cases … I dread these cases, and shudder every time a new one comes my way. Having taken it on, I feel I am living with a coffin tied to my back. It takes over my life, dominates my thoughts during the day, corrupts all pleasure and invades my dreams at night. I habitually have nightmares of executions, some of which I imagine are taking place in my apartment or just on the ledge outside the balcony.

In addition, most death row lawyers deal with the expectations of their clients as well as their families. Lastly, disclosure of unfavorable outcomes of the capital trial to clients and their families is yet another challenge faced by lawyers (Sheffer, 2013).

5.4.2 Experiences of Prison Staff and Execution Team

Research has analyzed varied reactions of the prison and execution staff toward the death row inmates. Studies have revealed that prison staff including prison wardens and guards often fear for their own safety around the death row prisoners whom they consider "dangerous." In addition, it is not uncommon for the prison staff to be distrustful of the prisoners and remain extra alert to avoid any form of mishap (Penal Reform International, 2015b). In Johnson's (2005) study, one prison officer expressed his constant stress thus

> They will hurt you to get away. You've got to watch them all the time. You know if these guys get a chance, you're gone. They'll kill you. They've all killed before. (p. 110)

[2]For an overview of this project visit https://www.albany.edu/scj/13189.php.

Due to the prolonged period of imprisonment and everyday interaction, some prison staff and death row inmates develop an empathetic relationship with each other. However, the bond formed between the prison staff and the death row prisoner may not be overtly displayed. Instead, the compassion may be suppressed and produce an internal conflict among the staff members, since their emotions are incongruent with their duty (Johnson, 2016). As a consequence of the same, the prison staff in regular contact with the death row inmates are generally not a part of the execution team (Johnson, 2016; Penal Reform International, 2015b). The execution process can bring up negative emotions among the execution team members, therefore, the entire task is broken down into smaller sections to make the entire routine as mechanical as possible. For instance, some personnel tie the leg and the others put a black cover on the head of the inmate (Adcock, 2010; Johnson, 2016). This diffuses the responsibility among the entire team and ensures that no one person can take the entire "blame" for an execution (Johnson, 2005). A qualitative analysis of 120 interviews conducted by Osofsky and Osofsky (2002) supported these assertions. The findings suggested that execution workers emphasized "caring professionalism" as an essential part of their job. In other words, the execution officers mentioned being highly professional in abiding by the rules and regulations of their job and at the same time in treating the death row inmate with respect (Osofsky & Osofsky, 2002). Based on these results, Osofsky et al. (2005) applied Bandura's (1990) Moral Disengagement Theory to explain the behavior of prison personnel involved in the execution process. According to this theory, moral disengagement involves.

> Cognitive restructuring of inhumane conduct into a benign or worthy one by moral justification, sanitizing language and exonerative social comparison; disavowal of personal agency in the harm one causes by diffusion or displacement of responsibility; disregarding or minimizing the injurious effects of one's actions; and attribution of blame to, and dehumanization of, those who are victimized (Bandura, 2002, p. 101).

Following this theory, prison personnel (see Fig. 5.1) may provide justifications for an execution such as maintenance of societal order and moral and religious

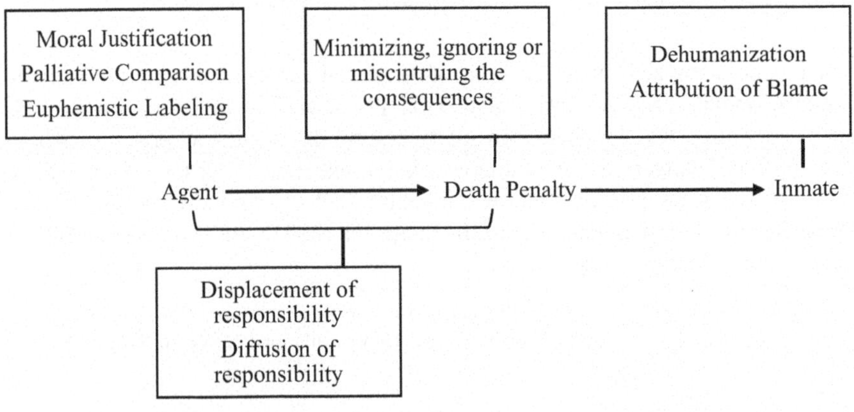

Fig. 5.1 Moral Disengagement Among Executioners (Bandura, 2008; Osofsky et al., 2005)

reasons. Prison officials may also use euphemistic language to comprehend taking the life of an individual and simply label it as a legal punishment for a heinous crime. Furthermore, prison personnel may diffuse the responsibility of the execution across various subsets of the judicial system and thus feel that their perceived responsibility for conducting the execution is lowered. Lastly, dehumanization and blaming a death row prisoner for the execution is also a way in which moral disengagement occurs among prison personnel (Bandura, 2008).

Osofsky et al. (2005) conducted an empirical study on 246 prison personnel using a 19-item scale to measure moral disengagement in prison personnel. The results revealed that moral disengagement among the participants was a function of the level of involvement in the execution process. Executioners were significantly higher on moral disengagement than the other groups who were not involved in the execution process (Osofsky et al., 2005).

Apart from this, not many empirical studies have been conducted using large samples of execution workers. Based on anecdotal experiences of executioners, researchers have suggested that being in an execution team can increase risk toward Post-Traumatic Stress Disorder like symptoms (Seemungal et al., 2016). According to Lifton and Mitchell (2000, p. 78), some execution team members face "executioner stress" which refers to the experience of insomnia, nightmares, depressive thoughts, and numbness. Some executioners and wardens advocated against the death penalty and published their experiences in memoirs. For instance, Donald Cabana's experiences were frequently cited in various articles and review papers (DeLilly, 2014; Gil et al., 2006; Mitchell, 2013; Seemungal et al., 2016). Cabana was a prison warden in Missouri in the 1980s. In his memoir *Death at Midnight: The Confession of an Executioner,* Cabana reported the psychological and physical impact of witnessing executions such as flashbacks of the event, avoidance of his warden duties, and three cardiac surgeries (DeLilly, 2014; Gil et al., 2006). Another case of John Ellis—an executioner—was widely covered by the media. Ellis was a part of a "botched" execution and died due to suicide in 1932. According to his son, Ellis had sleep difficulties and had flashbacks regarding the executions (Seemungal et al., 2016). In addition to the usage of PTSD to understand the experiences of executioners, DeLilly (2014) used the concept of Perpetration Induced Traumatic Stress (PITS). Although the symptomatology of PTSD and PITS is the same, the only difference is that in PITS the affected individual is an active perpetrator of the trauma that induced the stress (DeLilly, 2014).

5.4.3 Experiences of Execution Witnesses

In accordance with the law, certain individuals can witness an execution. These individuals may include executioners, medical specialists, journalists, volunteers and in some cases, families of victims and the death row prisoner.

Gil et al. (2006) in their review paper described studies conducted by Barnett (1995), and Freinkel, Koopman and Speigel (1994) which indicated the distress and dissociation (but not long-term trauma) among journalists who witnessed executions. Another review paper by Seemungal et al. (2016) presented the case of a public information director named Larry Fitzgerald, who witnessed 219 executions. Fitzgerald did not fully support death penalty and had nightmares regarding death row prisoners (Seemungal et al., 2016).

In some states, a victim's family has a right to view the execution of the accused. Some family members may want to watch the condemned die; however, in some cases they may choose to do so to adhere to the role of an "ideal" victim's family (Goodwin, 1997). This can be detrimental since researchers have argued that execution does not necessarily bring closure to a victim's family (Adcock, 2010; Bandes, 2009; Berns, 2009; Eaton & Christensen, 2014; Goodwin, 1997; Madeira, 2010). At times, executions do not go as planned, resulting in a dramatic and intensified suffering of the death row inmate. Witnessing such executions is associated with greater trauma (Johnson, 2016).

In rare cases, children may serve as a witness to an execution. For instance, in 2015 around 33 executions in Iran occurred in public places where children were also present. Consequently, there were reports of accidental deaths of children who attempted to re-enact execution scenes (Shaheed & Sanei, 2016). The limited research in this area highlights the enormous negative impact of witnessing executions.

5.5 Conclusion

The existing literature highlights the negative impact of death penalty on family members (of defendant and victim) and those who interact with death row prisoners. PTSD symptoms and grief are repeatedly noted among these groups. At the same time, it's important to consider that research in this area has several methodological limitations (Gil et al., 2006; Sharp, 2005; Vandiver & Berardo, 2000). Sharp (2005) described some of the limitations of the research pertaining to family members of capital defendants and victims. Studies in this area are mostly based on non-random and small samples that are selective, and mostly comprise of those relatives who are in contact with the death row prisoner. In addition, comparison of these family members with those of prisoners facing life sentences is lacking. The qualitative studies conducted in this area are mostly cross-sectional rather than longitudinal and thus the richness of the data collected is limited (Sharp, 2005). Therefore, the results of these studies are not generalizable (Vandiver & Berardo, 2000). In the case of jurors, lawyers, prison personnel, and execution witnesses, another set of limitations have been observed. Research on these groups is mostly based on limited systematic research, anecdotes, retrospective accounts, and memoirs (Gil et al., 2006). Therefore, further empirical research is required to understand the impact of death penalty on individuals who closely interact with the death row prisoners.

References

Adcock, C. F. (2010). The collateral anti-therapeutic effects of the death penalty. *Florida Coastal Law Review, 11*(2), 289–320.

American Psychiatric Association. (2013). *Diagnostic and statistical manual of mental disorders* (5th ed.). Arlington, VA: American Psychiatric Publishing.

Amick-McMullan, A., Kilpatrick, D. G., Veronen, L. J., & Smith, S. (1989). Family survivors of homicide victims: Theoretical perspectives and an exploratory study. *Journal of Traumatic Stress, 2*(1), 21–35.

Amick-McMullan, A., Kilpatrick, D. G., & Resnick, H. S. (1991). Homicide as a risk factor for PTSD among surviving family members. *Behavior Modification, 15*(4), 545–559.

Amnesty International. (2007). *The death penalty v. human rights: Why abolish the death penalty?* Retrieved from https://www.amnesty.org/en/documents/ACT51/002/2007/en/.

Antonio, M. E. (2006). I didn't know it'd be so hard-jurors' emotional reactions to serving on a capital trial. *Judicature, 89*(5), 282–288.

Antonio, M. E. (2008). Stress and the capital jury: How male and female jurors react to serving on a murder trial. *Justice System Journal, 29*(3), 396–407.

Armour, M. P. (2002). Journey of family members of homicide victims: A qualitative study of their posthomicide experience. *American Journal of Orthopsychiatry, 72*(3), 372.

Asaro, M. R. (2001). Working with adult homicide survivors, part I: Impact and sequelae of murder. *Perspectives in Psychiatric Care, 37*(3), 95–101.

Bandes, S. (2000). When victims seek closure: Forgiveness, vengeance and the role of government. *Fordham Urban Law Journal, 27*(5), 1599–1606.

Bandes, S. (2009). Victims, "closure", and the sociology of emotion. *Law and Contemporary Problems, 72*(2), 1–26.

Bandura, A. (1990). Selective activation and disengagement of moral control. *Journal of Social Issues, 46*(1), 27–46.

Bandura, A. (2002). Selective moral disengagement in the exercise of moral agency. *Journal of moral education, 31*(2), 101–119.

Bandura, A. (2008). Moral disengagement in state executions. In B. L. Cutler (Ed.), *Encyclopedia of psychology and law* (pp. 515–518). Thousand Oaks, CA: Sage Publications.

Barnett, C. (1995). Covering executions. *American Journalism Review, 17*, 27–39.

Beck, E., Blackwell, B. S., Leonard, P. B., & Mears, M. (2002). Seeking sanctuary: Interviews with family members of capital defendants. *Cornell Law Review, 88*(2), 382–418.

Berns, N. (2009). Contesting the victim card: Closure discourse and emotion in death penalty rhetoric. *The Sociological Quarterly, 50*(3), 383–406.

Bienen, L. B. (1992). Helping jurors out: Post-verdict debriefing for jurors in emotionally disturbing trials. *Indiana Law Journal, 68*(4), 1333–1355.

Burns, J. L. (2006). Families of homicide victims speak: An examination of perceptions of the criminal justice system and capital punishment (Doctoral dissertation, Oklahoma State University). Retrieved from https://digital.library.okstate.edu/etd/umi-okstate-1785.pdf.

Chinni, D., & Grier, P. (2001, June 11). For survivors, execution isn't the end. *The Christian Science Monitor.* Retrieved from https://www.csmonitor.com/2001/0611/p1s2.html.

Death Penalty Information Center. (2015). *International polls and studies*. Retrieved from https://deathpenaltyinfo.org/international-polls-and-studies-0.

DeLilly, L. M. (2014). Antithetical to human dignity: Secondary trauma, evolving standards of decency, and the unconstitutional consequences of state-sanctioned executions. *Southern California Interdisciplinary Law Journal, 23*, 107–145.

Doka, K. J. (1989). Disenfranchised grief. In K. J. Doka (Ed.), *Disenfranchised grief: Recognizing hidden sorrow* (pp. 3–11). Lexington, MA: Lexington Books.

Eaton, J., & Christensen, T. (2014). Closure and its myths: Victims' families, the death penalty, and the closure argument. *International Review of Victimology, 20*(3), 327–343.

Eschholz, S., Reed, M. D., Beck, E., & Leonard, P. B. (2003). Offenders' family members' responses to capital crimes: The need for restorative justice initiatives. *Homicide studies, 7*(2), 154–181.

Freinkel, A., Koopman, C., & Speigel, D. (1994). Dissociative symptoms in media eyewitnesses of an execution. *American Journal of Psychiatry, 151*(9), 1335–1339.

Gil, A., Johnson, M. B., & Johnson, I. (2006). Secondary trauma associated with state executions: Testimony regarding execution procedures. *The Journal of Psychiatry & Law, 34*(1), 25–35.

Goodwin, M. L. (1997). An eyeful for an eye-an argument against allowing the families of murder victims to view executions. *Brandeis Journal of Family Law, 36*(4), 585–608.

Hood, R., & Hoyle, C. (2009). Abolishing the death penalty worldwide: The impact of a "new dynamic". *Crime and Justice, 38*(1), 1–63.

Johnson, R. (2005). *Death work a study of the modern execution process* (2nd ed.). Belmont, CA: Wadsworth Publishing.

Johnson, R. (2016). Executioners at work: Collateral consequences of executions for officers working on death row and in the death house. In I. Šimonović (Ed.), *Death penalty and the victims* (pp. 307–324). New York: United Nations Human Rights. Retrieved from https://www.ohchr.org/EN/newyork/Documents/Death-Penalty-and-the-Victims-WEB.PDF.

Jones, S. J., & Beck, E. (2007). Disenfranchised grief and nonfinite loss as experienced by the families of death row inmates. *OMEGA-Journal of Death and Dying, 54*(4), 281–299.

King, R. (2003). *Don't kill in our names: Families of murder victims speak out against the death penalty*. New Jersey, USA: Rutgers University Press.

King, K. (2004). It hurts so bad: Comparing grieving patterns of the families of murder victims with those of families of death row inmates. *Criminal Justice Policy Review, 15*(2), 193–211.

King, R. (2006). The impact of capital punishment on families of defendants and murder victims' family members. *Judicature, 89*(5), 292–296.

King, R., & Norgard, K. (1999). What about our families-using the impact on death row defendants' family members as a mitigating factor in death penalty sentencing hearings. *Florida State University Law Review, 26*(4), 1119–1176.

Kübler-Ross, E. (1969). *On death and dying*. New York, USA: Scribner.

Lacock, T., & Radelet, M. (2009). Do executions lower homicide rates?: The views of leading criminologists. *Journal of Criminal Law & Criminology, 99*(2), 489–508.

Lifton, R. J., & Mitchell, G. (2000). *Who owns death? Capital punishment, the American conscience, and the end of executions*. New York: Harper Collins.

Logan, W. A. (1999). Declaring life at the crossroads of death: Victims' anti-death penalty views and prosecutors' charging decisions. *Criminal Justice Ethics, 18*(2), 41–57.

Madeira, J. L. (2010). "Why rebottle the genie?": Capitalizing on closure in death penalty proceedings. *Indiana Law Journal, 85*(4), 1477–1525.

Mitchell, P. (2013, October 25). The weight of capital punishment on jurors, justices, governors, & executioners. *Verdict*. Retrieved from https://verdict.justia.com/2013/10/25/weight-capital-punishment-jurors-justices-governors-executioners.

Nicolau, I. (2013). Historical evolution of the death penalty abolition as a fundamental human right. *Contemporary Readings in Law and Social Justice, 5*(2), 278.

Osofsky, M. J., & Osofsky, H. J. (2002). The psychological experience of security officers who work with executions. *Psychiatry, 65*(4), 358–370.

Osofsky, M. J., Bandura, A., & Zimbardo, P. G. (2005). The role of moral disengagement in the execution process. *Law and Human Behavior, 29*(4), 371–393.

Penal Reform International. (2014). *Fighting for clients' lives: The impact of the death penalty on defence lawyers*. Retrieved from https://www.penalreform.org/wp-content/uploads/2014/04/fighting-for-clients-v3-web.pdf.

Penal Reform International. (2015a). *UN Secretary-General's 2015 report to the Human Rights Council on the death penalty Submission by Penal Reform International (PRI)*. Retrieved from https://www.penalreform.org/wp-content/uploads/2015/06/Wider-impacts-of-the-death-penalty-submission-to-UN-Secretary-General-annual-report.pdf.

Penal Reform International. (2015b). *Prison guards and the death penalty*. Retrieved from https://www.penalreform.org/wp-content/uploads/2015/04/PRI-Prison-guards-briefing-paper.pdf.

Radelet, M. L., & Borg, M. J. (2000). The changing nature of death penalty debates. *Annual Review of Sociology, 26*(1), 43–61.

Rainer, J. (2013). *Life after loss: Contemporary grief counseling and therapy*. Eau Claire, USA: PESI Publishing & Media.

Robertson, O., & Brett, R. (2013). *Lightening the load of the parental death penalty on children*. Quaker United Nations Office.

Seemungal, F., Seal, L., & Black, L. (2016). Death penalty and its impact on the professionals involved in the execution process. In I. Šimonović (Ed.), *Death penalty and the victims* (pp. 295–306). New York: United Nations Human Rights. Retrieved from https://www.ohchr.org/EN/newyork/Documents/Death-Penalty-and-the-Victims-WEB.PDF.

Shaheed, A., & Sanei, F. (2016). Outlier: Iran and its use of the death penalty. In I. Šimonović (Ed.), *Death penalty and the victims* (pp. 181–209). New York: United Nations Human Rights. Retrieved from https://www.ohchr.org/EN/newyork/Documents/Death-Penalty-and-the-Victims-WEB.PDF.

Sharp, S. F. (2005). *Hidden victims: The effects of the death penalty on families of the accused*. New Jersey, USA: Rutgers University Press.

Sharp, S. F. (2016). Hidden victims: The families of those facing the death penalty. In I. Šimonović (Ed.), *Death penalty and the victims* (pp. 222–235). New York: United Nations Human Rights. Retrieved from https://www.ohchr.org/EN/newyork/Documents/Death-Penalty-and-the-Victims-WEB.PDF.

Sheffer, S. (2013). *Fighting for their lives: Inside the experience of capital defense attorneys*. Nashville: Vanderbilt University Press.

Ssuubi, F. (2016). The impact of the death penalty on the children with a parent on death row or executed. In I. Šimonović (Ed.), *Death penalty and the victims* (pp. 236–251). New York: United Nations Human Rights. Retrieved from https://www.ohchr.org/EN/newyork/Documents/Death-Penalty-and-the-Victims-WEB.PDF.

United Nations Human Rights Council. (2012). *Moving away from the death penalty: Lessons from national experience*. Retrieved from https://www.ohchr.org/Lists/MeetingsNY/Attachments/27/moving_away_from_death_penalty_web.pdf.

United Nations Human Rights Council. (2013, July 24). *Question of the death penalty—Report of the Secretary-General* (Report no: A/HRC/24/18). Retrieved from https://undocs.org/en/A/HRC/24/18.

Vandiver, M. (1998). The impact of the death penalty on the families of homicide victims and of condemned prisoners. In J. R. Acker, R. M. Bohm, & C. S. Lanier (Eds.), *America's experiment with capital punishment: Reflections on the past, present, and future of the ultimate penal sanction* (pp. 477–505). Durham, NC: Carolina Academic Press.

Vandiver, M., & Berardo, F. M. (2000). 'It's like dying every day': The families of condemned prisoners. *Families, Crime and Criminal Justice, 2*, 339–358.

Zhigang, Y. (2009). Abolition or retention: Rethinking the death penalty in China. *Social Sciences in China, 30*(2), 178–190.

Zinzow, H. M., Rheingold, A. A., Hawkins, A. O., Saunders, B. E., & Kilpatrick, D. G. (2009). Losing a loved one to homicide: Prevalence and mental health correlates in a national sample of young adults. *Journal of Traumatic Stress, 22*(1), 20–27.

Chapter 6
Public Opinion on Death Penalty: An Indian Study

6.1 Introduction

In India, death penalty is given in the rarest of rare cases by the court. Death penalty can be imposed only in the gravest cases taking into account the aggravating and mitigating circumstances of the case and paying due regard to the circumstances of the offence. In addition to the judicial system, views of general citizens of the country also contribute toward the retention or rejection of capital punishment. In the past, several countries have cited public opinion as a reason to retain death penalty (e.g., Taiwan, Belarus, and USA) (Hood, 2015; UN General Assembly, 2010; Butler, Unnever, Cullen, & Thielo, 2017). Those taking the retentionist stance draw upon the argument that lack of public support undermines the general confidence in the criminal justice system (Hood, 2015). A recent example of this occurred in India, where mass protests after the rape of a minor acted as a catalyst in the President's assent to the ordinance which included death penalty as a punishment for rape of female minors (Express Web Desk, 2018a). Overall, public opinion significantly impacts policies and legislations (Burstein, 2003; Epstein, 2012). Therefore, public opinion offers valuable insights in understanding the death penalty trends and the abolitionist/retentionist stance of a country (see Chap. 4 for detailed information).

There is less research on the opinion of Indian citizens on death penalty (Lambert et al., 2016). Most of the public opinion polls in India have been conducted by newspaper agencies and are limited to single close-ended questions (yes or no) (see Times of India, 2018; Jha, 2013). Moreover, the few research studies published in this area (Kamble & Mullet, 2014; Lambert et al., 2016; Lambert, Pasupuleti, Jiang, Jaishankar, & Bhimarasetty, 2008) utilized samples of Indian college students, and thus the results cannot be generalized as belonging to the entire Indian population. To address these gaps in literature, a study was conducted by the Jindal Institute of Behavioural Sciences in India (n = 25,210) to understand the opinion of public on the death penalty. The chapter is based on this research and presents a detailed description of the study's aims, methods used, major findings, and discussion of the results.

S. P. Sahni and M. Junnarkar, *The Death Penalty*,
https://doi.org/10.1007/978-981-15-3129-3_6

6.2 Aim of the Public Opinion Study

The aim of the study was to gather a detailed understanding of public perception of death penalty in India. Research indicates that opinions of citizens on death penalty vary according to factors such as demographic variables (like age, gender, and education qualification), social values, and beliefs. Therefore, the aims of the present study were to understand

(a) the perception of public in India toward death penalty;
(b) the reasons for support/opposition of death penalty;
(c) the type of crime and circumstances for which death penalty is favored; and
(d) the demographic correlates of the public opinion on death penalty.

6.3 Method

6.3.1 Sample

The demographic details of the participants of this study (N = 25,210) are as follows.

6.3.1.1 Age and Gender

The sample for this study comprised of 25,210 participants (males = 14,100, females = 9,515 females) in the age range of 12–80 years (Mean age = 29.76, SD = 12.63) (see Figs. 6.1 and 6.2). For the purpose of analysis, five age groups were formulated according to developmental age range: 12–18 years (males = 766, females = 817), 19–25 years (males = 3049, females = 3160), 26–35 years (males = 2800, females = 1766), 36–45 years (males = 3458, females = 1713), and 45 years and above (males = 3537, females = 1687). Maximum participants belonged to the 19–25 age range (n = 6598, 27.3%) and minimum belonged to the 12–18 years age group (n = 1695, 7%). There were more male (59.71%) participants than females (40.29%) and the gender distribution of the sample closely approximates the sex ratio in India (943 females: 1000 males) (Census of India, 2011a).

6.3.1.2 Educational Qualification

Majority (n = 10,731, 43.36%) of the participants had a postgraduate degree or an undergraduate degree (n = 6432, 25.5%) as their highest educational qualification. Very few participants were Ph.D. holders (719, 2.9%) or had a qualification of 10th class (n = 1735, 6.9%) or lower (n = 1254, 5%) (Fig. 6.3).

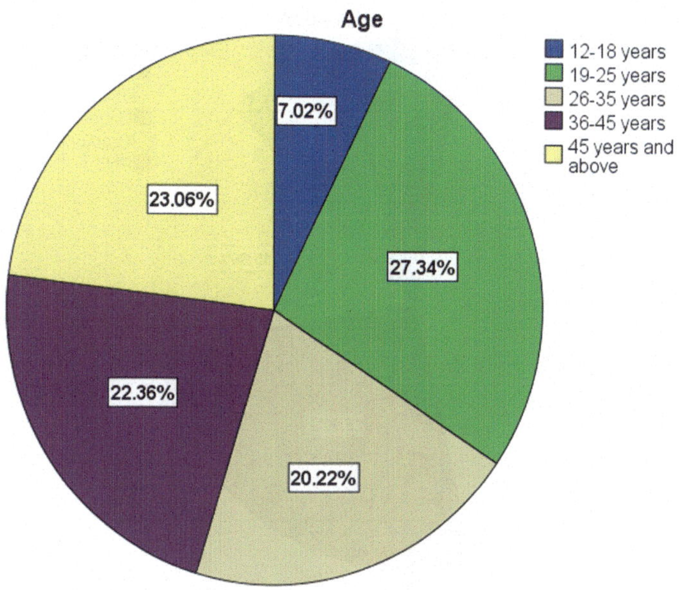

Fig. 6.1 Distribution of participants according to their age group

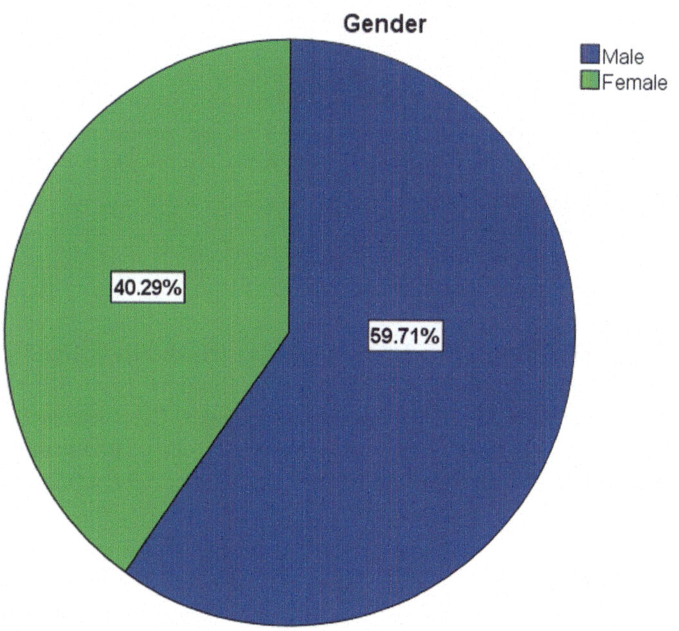

Fig. 6.2 Distribution of participants according to their gender

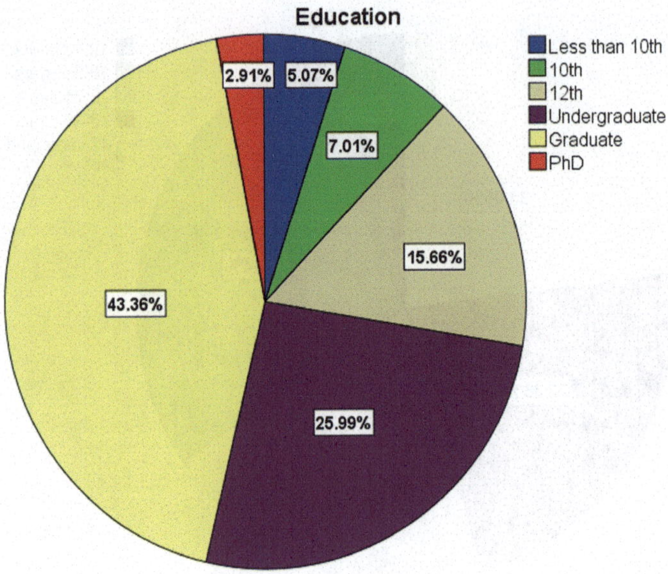

Fig. 6.3 Distribution of participants according to their educational qualification

6.3.1.3 Profession

The sample was almost equally represented by businessman/self-employed persons (n = 7571, 30.76%), students (n = 6854, 27.84%), and professionals (n = 5350, 21.73%), whereas homemakers (n = 2698, 10.96%) and others (n = 2144, 8.71%) were in minority (Fig. 6.4).

6.3.1.4 Religion

Majority of the participants identified themselves as Hindus (n = 18,473, 74.66%) and the least number of participants belonged to Buddhist (n = 328, 1.33%) or religions other than (n = 0.43%) Hindu, Muslim, Sikh, Christian, and Jain. This was expected since in comparison to other religious groups, Hinduism is the most populous and widespread group in India (Census of India, 2011b) (Fig. 6.5).

6.3.1.5 Economic Status

With respect to the economic status, participants each of the income groups, namely, less than Rs. 20,000 (n = 5355, 23.51%) Rs. 20,000–50,000 (n = 4891, 21.47%), Rs. 50,000–1,00,000 (n = 5614, 24.65%), and Rs. 1,00,000 and above (n = 6917, 30.37%) were similarly represented in the sample (Fig. 6.6).

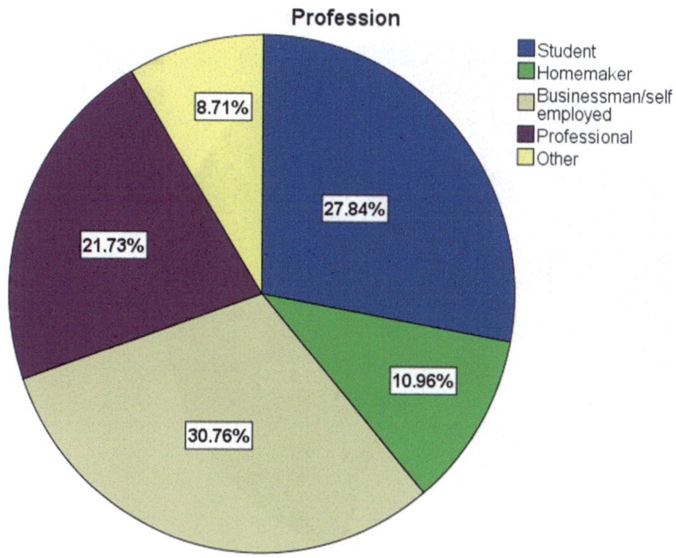

Fig. 6.4 Distribution of participants according to their profession

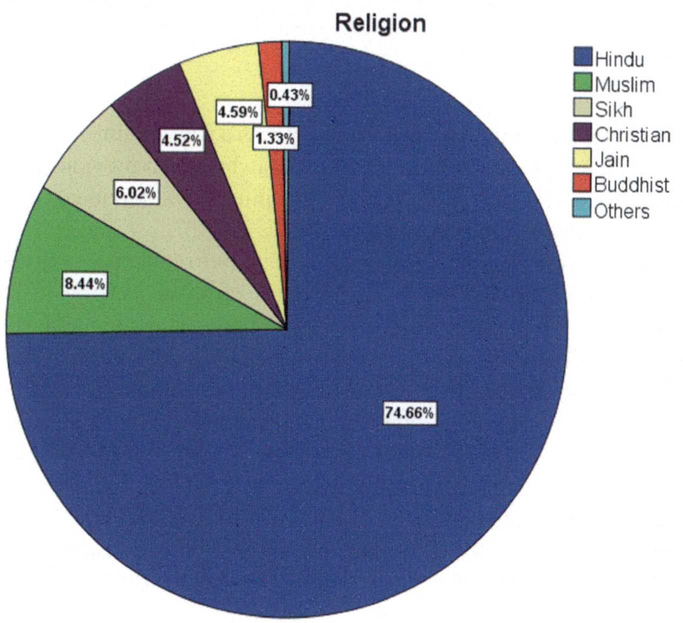

Fig. 6.5 Distribution of participants according to their religion

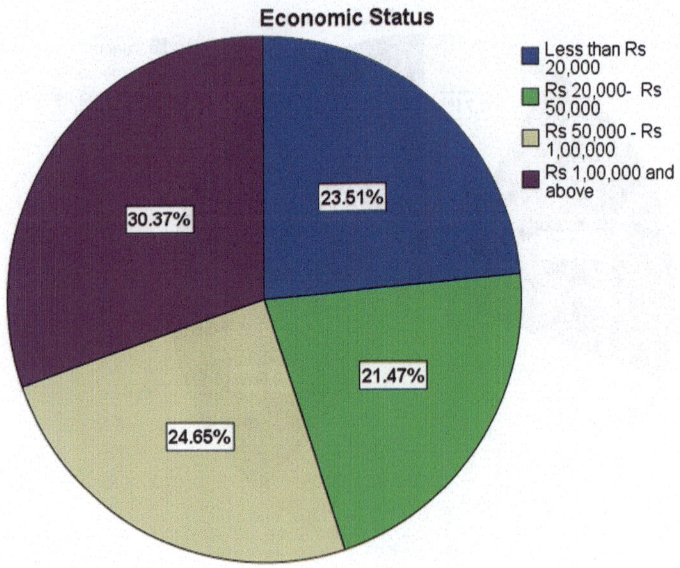

Fig. 6.6 Distribution of participants according to their monthly income

6.3.2 Measure

The survey questionnaire utilized for this study was a self-administered survey that comprised of 17 questions. The questionnaire was based on previous literature on public opinion on death penalty. To explore the opinions of individuals in depth, the questionnaire was divided into three parts.

The first section (Questions 1–8) comprised of items to collect demographic information and the basic opinion of the participants on death penalty in India. The demographic details in the survey included age, gender (male, female), educational qualification (less than 10th, 10th, 12th, undergraduate, graduate, Ph.D.), profession (student, homemaker, business/self-employed, professional, other), religion (Hindu, Muslim, Sikh, Christian, Jain, Buddhist, other), and economic status (less than Rs. 20,000 per month, Rs. 20,000–50,000 per month, Rs. 50,000–1,00,000 per month, above Rs. 1,00,000 per month). The last question in this section asked the participants "Do you want death penalty to remain legalized?". Participants who gave a "yes" response were instructed to answer only Part A of the questionnaire and those who chose "no" as their response were directed to answer only Part B.

6.3.2.1 Part A: Reasons for Support and Crimes for Which Death Penalty Should Be Legal

The participants who indicated support for death penalty completed questions 9–11. The questions asked participants to report reasons for their support toward death penalty (eye for an eye, acts as a deterrent, proportionate to the wrong done); the crimes for which death penalty should be a legal punishment (e.g., murder, rape, treason, offences against children, dowry death); and lastly three subparts of question 11 inquired in what way and whether death penalty would help a victim's family.

6.3.2.2 Part B: Reasons for Abolishing Death Penalty

The questions 12–16 explored the reasons for supporting abolishment of death penalty. Question 12 asked about why death penalty should be abolished and included options such as violates right to life, unproductive results, uneconomical, biased decision-making against the accused, barbaric, and inhumane. Questions 13 and 14 further tapped into the reasons for supporting abolishment by asking respondents to indicate whether they agree or disagree with certain statements provided.

6.3.3 Data Collection and Data Screening

For this study, data were collected randomly using a death penalty survey that was developed specifically for this research. Data collection occurred over 60 days through online and offline methods. Out of the data collected, the forms that were less than 35% complete or blank were rejected. In total, 10% of the forms were rejected and 25,210 (M = 14,100, F = 9,515) responses were finally considered for the descriptive analysis.

6.4 Results

6.4.1 Public Opinion on Death Penalty

Participants were posed with the question "Do you want death penalty to remain legalized?" to capture the broad support of the public toward death penalty. Overall, 80% (n = 20,163) of the participants indicated support for death penalty and 20% (n = 5047) were not in favor of its legalization. These results point toward a strong support for death penalty among the public in India. However, limited research on the level of support toward death penalty in India showed that there is no clear opposition or support of capital punishment among the public. Lambert et al. (2008)

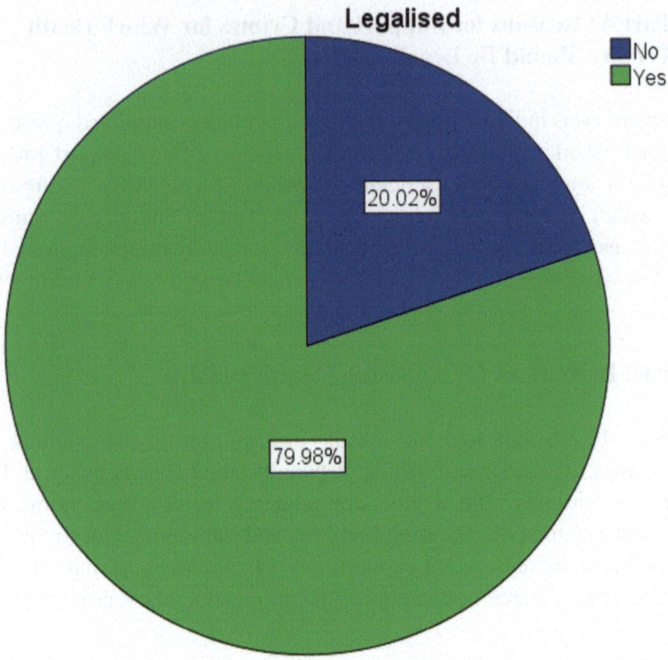

Fig. 6.7 Public opinion on legalization of death penalty

used a seven-point Likert scale to understand the opinion of Indian college students (N = 434) on death penalty. Findings indicated almost equal support (43%) and opposition (44%) for death penalty. Similar results were obtained by Lambert and his colleagues (2016) in a comparative study of Indian and US college students (N = 918) on death penalty support. The findings of this research were based on a larger sample (N = 25,210) with individuals from varied groups (age, education levels, profession, and so on), whereas the samples in the previous studies only consisted of college students and could be a reason for the differing results obtained in this study (Fig. 6.7).

The responses of participants on this item were further analyzed with respect to all the demographic variables (age, gender, educational qualification, profession, religion, and economic status) and the results are presented in the sections that follow.

6.4.1.1 Age and Gender

There was a steady increase with age in the number of participants who supported the legalization of death penalty (see Fig. 6.8). Literature from Western countries also highlights that older individuals are likely to have stronger support for death penalty than younger individuals (Fox, Radelet, & Bonsteel, 1990; Vollum, Longmire, & Buffington-Vollum, 2004). Stack (2004) found that age influenced death penalty

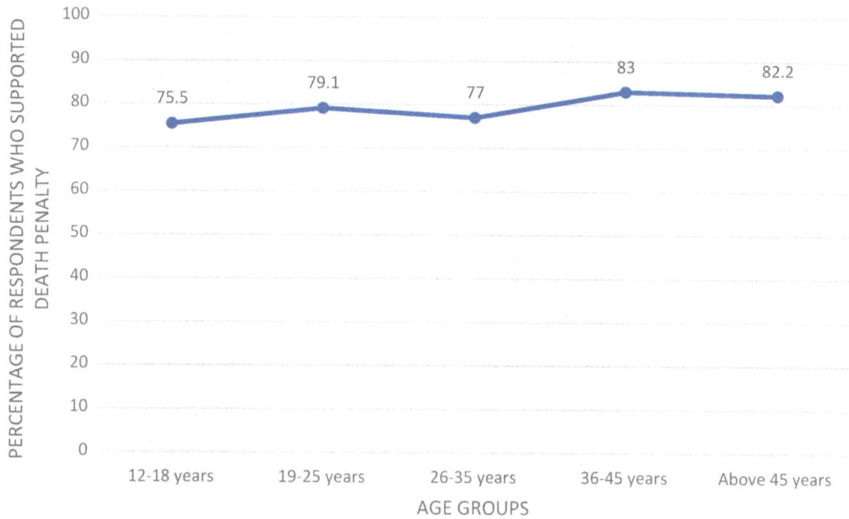

Fig. 6.8 Distribution of respondents who supported death penalty according to age group

support since it is positively associated with punitiveness. However, the study on death penalty support conducted by Lambert et al. (2008) in India revealed that age had no significant correlation with the opinions of the participants. Therefore, more research is required to explore the association between age and death penalty support in India.

In case of gender, the broad support for death penalty did not vary much between males [Yes (n) = 11,457, 81.2%, No (n) = 2,643, 18.8%] and females [Yes (n) = 7424, 78% No (n) = 2091, 22%]. A gender gap (males are more likely to favor) in death penalty support has been observed in Western (Baumer, Messner, & Rosenfeld, 2003; Miller & Hayward, 2008; Stack, 2000, 2004; Vollum, Longmire, & Buffington-Vollum, 2004) and Indian studies (Lambert et al., 2008; Lambert et al., 2016). In India, one study found that in a sample of college students, 57% males favored death penalty in comparison to 27% of females (Lambert et al., 2016). However, Applegate, Cullen and Fisher (2002) emphasized that in most studies the difference in opinion among males and females does not imply that they have opposing views but rather a difference in their degree of support (as cited in Sato, 2013). Previous research by Lambert et al. (2008) and Lambert et al. (2016) in India utilized a seven-point Likert scale to measure the level of death penalty support. This may be a better alternative to the dichotomous scale used in the present study to test Applegate and his colleagues' hypothesis.

Cross-tabulation of the public opinion on legalization of death penalty with age and gender revealed that with age there was a steady increase in the support of males toward death penalty (76%, 78.6%, 77.9%, 84.9%, 83.4%) (see Fig. 6.9). Figure 6.10 indicates that in younger age groups (i.e., 12–18 years and 19–25 years) both males and females equally support death penalty; however, in the middle age and older age

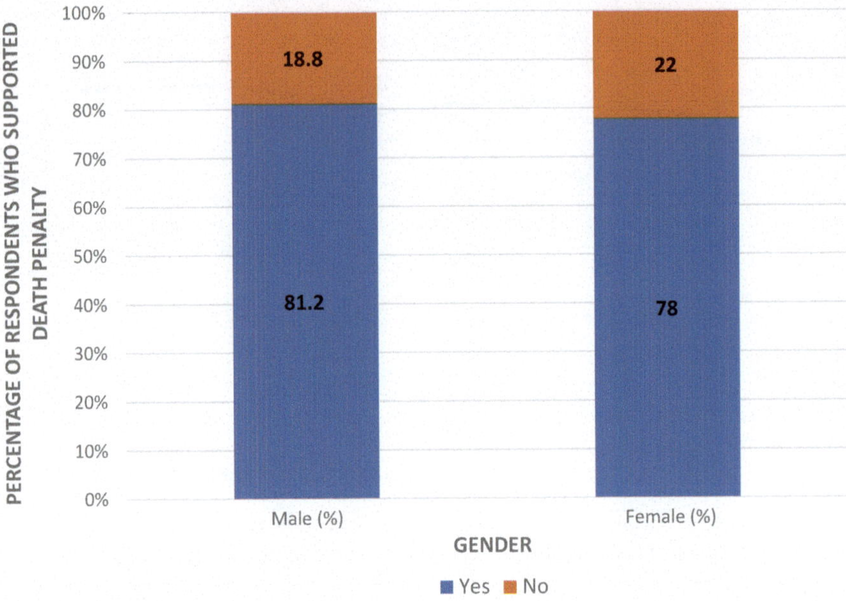

Fig. 6.9 Distribution of respondents who supported death penalty according to their gender

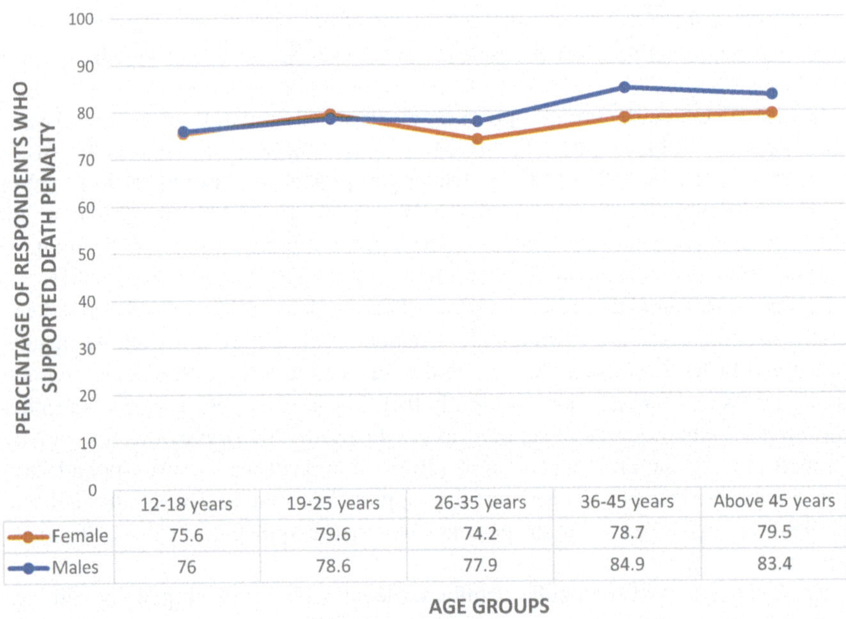

	12-18 years	19-25 years	26-35 years	36-45 years	Above 45 years
Female	75.6	79.6	74.2	78.7	79.5
Males	76	78.6	77.9	84.9	83.4

Fig. 6.10 Distribution of male and female respondents who supported death penalty according to their age groups

groups (26–35 years, 36–45 years, above 45 years), males more strongly supported legalization of death penalty (77.9%, 84.9%, 83.4%, respectively) than their female counterparts (74.2%, 78.7%, 79.5%, respectively). This interaction between age and gender can be further explored in future studies.

6.4.1.2 Educational Qualification

There was a decrease in support toward death penalty legalization with advancement in educational qualification (less than 10th: 86.8%, 10th class: 82.5%, 12th class: 81.3%, undergraduate: 80.5%, graduate: 78.3%, Ph.D.: 75%) (see Fig. 6.11 for trend). A similar decreasing trend was observed in the support of death penalty among males. Among both males (less than 10th: 87.6%, 10th class: 84.9%, 12th class: 84.9%, undergraduate: 81.9%, graduate: 78.2%, Ph.D.: 75.2%) and females (less than 10th: 82.4%, 10th class: 79.5%, 12th class: 75.7%, undergraduate: 78.3%, graduate: 78%, Ph.D.: 75.3%), this trend was evident. Previous public opinion studies conducted in India (Lambert et al., 2008) included only college students as participants; therefore, the relationship between educational qualification and death penalty support has not been comprehensively explored. Nevertheless, research in other countries similarly demonstrated that with increase in educational level, support for death penalty reduces (Fox, Radelet, & Bonsteel, 1990). For instance, Widony and Hammer (2009) used data of 2201 respondents from the 2006 General Social Survey and

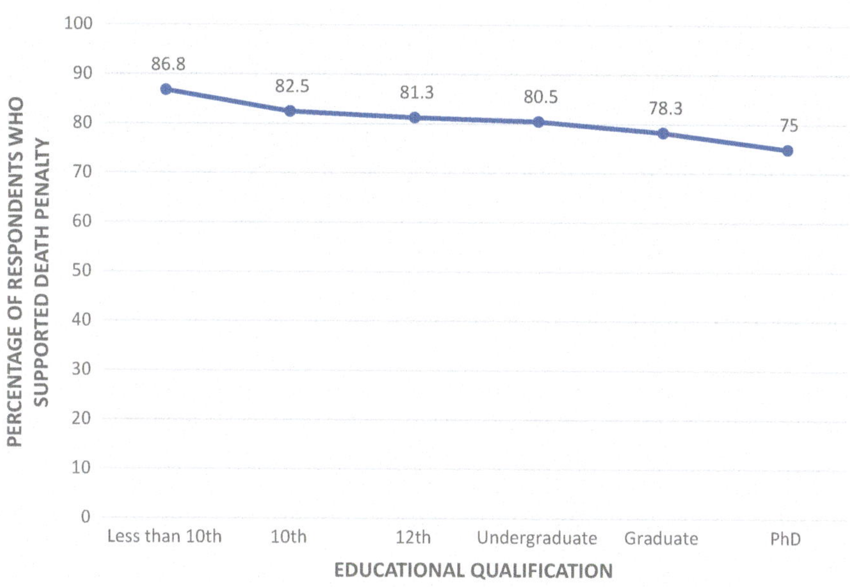

Fig. 6.11 Distribution of respondents who supported death penalty according to their educational qualification

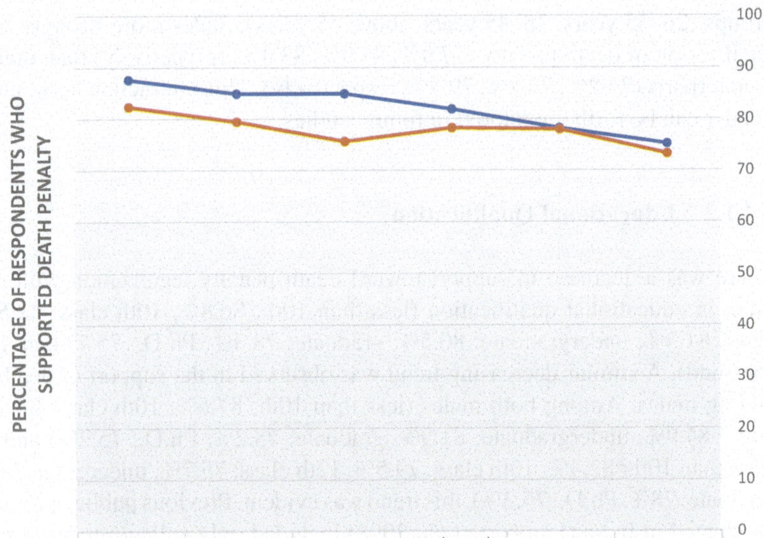

	Less than 10th	10th	12th	Undergraduate	Graduate	PhD
Males yes (%)	87.6	84.9	84.9	81.9	78.2	75.2
Females yes (%)	82.4	79.5	75.7	78.3	78	73.3

Fig. 6.12 Distribution of male and female respondents who supported death penalty according to their educational qualification

found that death penalty was favored by 78.1% of those who completed high school, 64.4% of those who held Bachelor's degree, and 56.3% of those with a graduate degree. It is probable that with increase in academic qualification, the knowledge regarding death penalty and related debates improves, thus leading to a decline in the death penalty support. On similar lines, Fox, Radelet and Bonsteel (1990) suggested that one way to change the public opinion about death penalty is to educate the people about how the criminal justice system works in a country (Fig. 6.12).

6.4.1.3 Profession

It was observed that similar percentage of students (78.9%), homemakers (78.4%), and self-employed (78%) and professionals (81.8%) individuals supported the legalization of death penalty (see Fig. 6.13). Genderwise analysis showed that greater percentage of male homemakers and self-employed individuals (86% and 79.5%, respectively) supported legalization of death penalty than their female counterparts (76.6% and 72.4%, respectively) (see Fig. 6.14). Unlike other demographic variables, there is not enough support for the association between occupation and opinion on death penalty. Studies that examined the association between occupation and death penalty opinions have yielded mixed results. Some like Bohm (1991) upon analysis of Gallup polls found that manual laborers were less likely to favor death penalty than

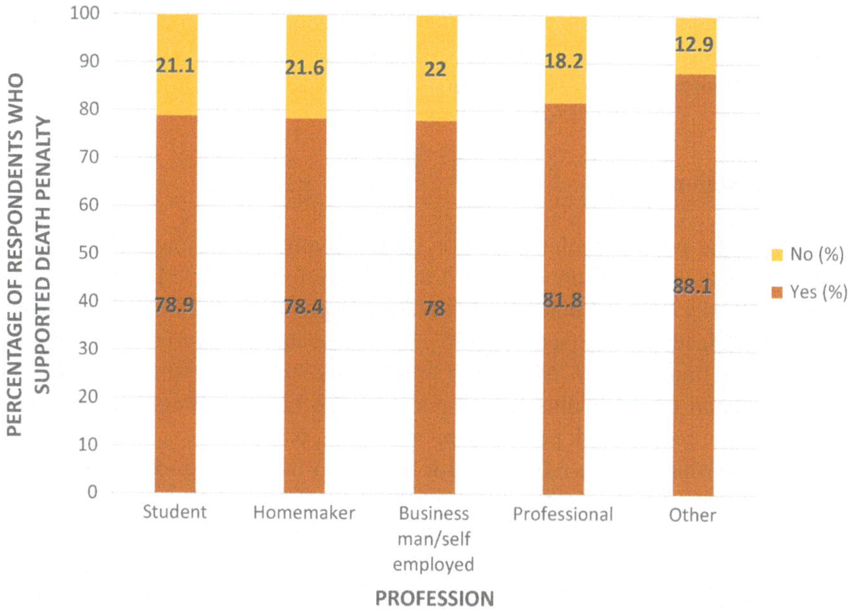

Fig. 6.13 Distribution of respondents who supported death penalty according to their profession

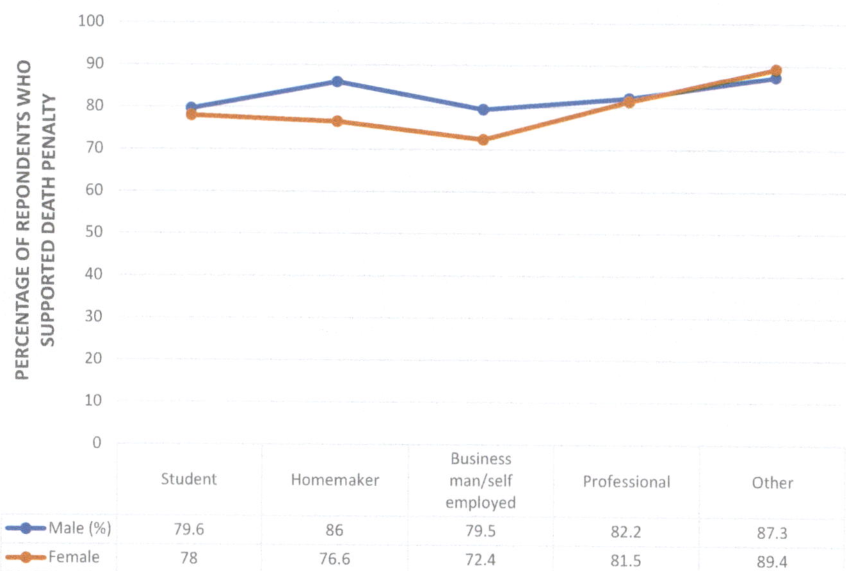

Fig. 6.14 Distribution of male and female respondents who supported death penalty according to their profession

clerical and sales professionals. Others like Vidmar and Ellsworth (1974) reviewed studies that did not reflect significant differences in opinions of businesspersons, white-collar workers, farmers, and manual laborers.

6.4.1.4 Religion

Analysis of the public opinion based on religious affiliation showed that Hindus (81.8%) were the greatest supporters of death penalty, followed by Muslims (78.7%) and Sikhs (77.4%). On the other hand, Buddhist respondents (65.5%) were the least supportive of death penalty (see Fig. 6.15). It was also interesting to note that among all religions (Hindus 78.4%, Muslims 73.6%, Sikhs 70.8%, Christians 61.3%, and Jains 67%) apart from Buddhism, respondents in the 12–18 year age group formed the least proportion of death penalty supporters (Fig. 6.16).

The relationship between religion and death penalty has been explored extensively. Since each religion presents its own understanding of life, death, punishment, and morality, researchers have used this variable to comprehend death penalty attitudes of the public. For instance, the *Sharia* law traditionally prescribes death penalty for five offences which include murder and four *hudud* crimes (adultery, murder, apostasy, sodomy) (Alasti & Bronson, 2017). In Christianity as well, death penalty supporters often quote *lextalionis* or law of retaliation from the Bible, according to which if

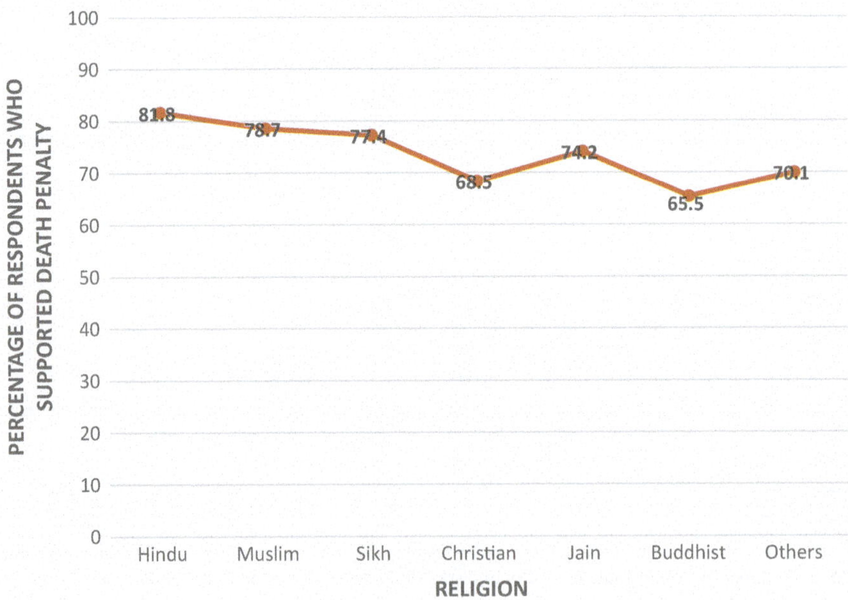

Fig. 6.15 Distribution of respondents who supported death penalty according to their religious affiliation

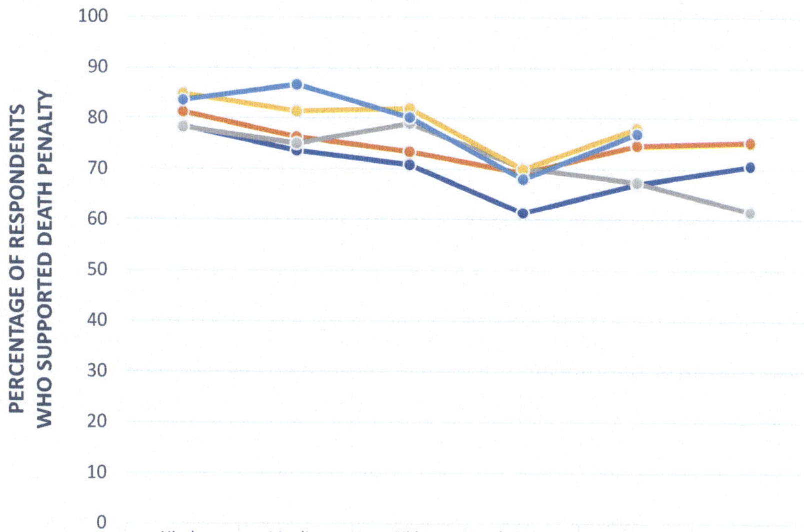

	Hindu	Muslim	Sikh	Christian	Jain	Buddhist
12-18 years	78.4	73.6	70.8	61.3	67	70.6
19-25 years	81.2	76.3	73.4	69.2	74.6	75.3
26-35 years	78.2	75	78.9	70.2	67.3	61.5
36-45 years	84.8	81.4	81.9	70	78	
Above 45 years	83.5	86.6	80.1	68	76.9	

RELIGION

Fig. 6.16 Distribution of respondents who supported death penalty according to their religious affiliation

harm is done then one shall give life for life, eye for eye, and tooth for tooth (Winright, 2017). Therefore, religion may act as a key variable in understanding public opinion on death penalty. Contrary to this expectation, Lambert et al. (2008) study in India indicated that there was no significant difference between the opinion on death penalty among Hindus and non-Hindus. Another study conducted in India by Kamble and Mullet (2014) supported that people from Hindu religion did not differ from the others (Muslims, Christian, Jain) in their judgements about the appropriateness of death penalty under varying circumstances. However, in the current study, there is a considerable difference (approximately 16%) between the death penalty support indicated by Hindu and Buddhist participants. The previous studies in India (Kamble & Mullet, 2014; Lambert et al., 2008) grouped all non-Hindu religions together and thus did not explore the differences in death penalty support among various religious groups in detail. Therefore, the relationship between religion and death penalty support among the Indian population requires further research.

6.4.1.5 Economic Status

Figure 6.17 indicates that those in the income group of Rs. 20,000–50,000 supported legalization of death penalty in the greatest proportion (84.5%), whereas those earning between Rs. 50,000–1,00,000 per month supported death penalty in comparatively lesser numbers (75.8%). Males and females across various income groups followed a similar trend in support for death penalty (see Fig. 6.18). Therefore, no specific trends were revealed for this variable. Even previous research examining the relationship between income and death penalty attitude has provided mixed results (Sato, 2013). Baumer, Messner and Rosenfeld (2003) found that in addition to those with low income, individuals living in low-income areas[1] were also less likely to support death penalty. On the other hand, Stack (2004) instead found support for the inverse relationship[2] and Young's (1991) research indicated that high-income levels were associated with death penalty support only among whites.

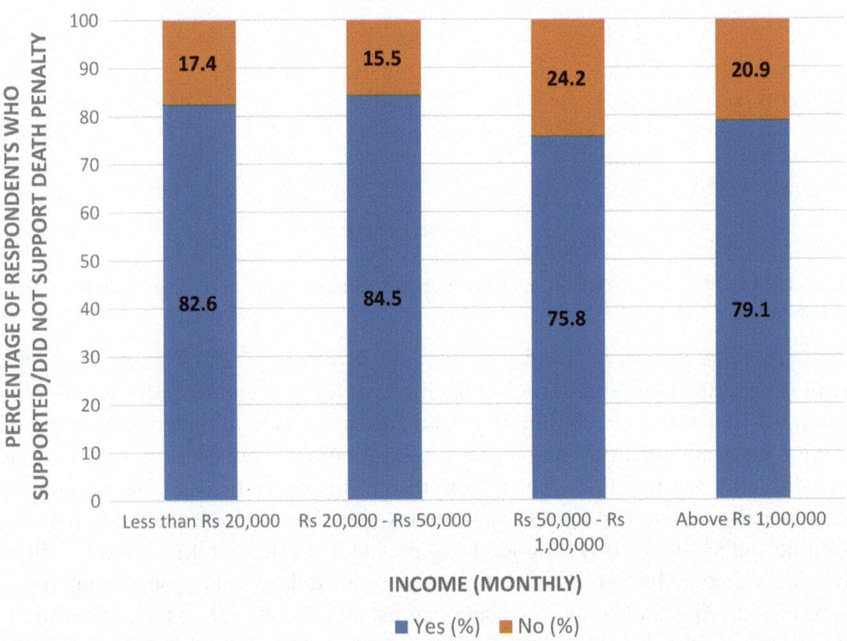

Fig. 6.17 Distribution of respondents who supported death penalty according to their monthly income

[1]Family income and other individual and contextual variables were controlled to compute this result.

[2]Those with high income were less likely to support death penalty.

Fig. 6.18 Distribution of male and female respondents who supported death penalty according to their monthly income

6.4.2 Support for Death Penalty

Responses provided to items in Part A of the survey revealed the reasons for which participants supported the legalization of death penalty and the crimes for which death penalty should be legalized. Results are presented below in percentages. In addition, cross-tabulations were made to understand the results with respect to the demographic variables.

6.4.2.1 Reasons for Support

Most number of respondents indicated that giving death penalty was justified since this punishment is "proportionate to the wrong done" (43.1%) and that it acts as a deterrent for future crimes (39.1%).[3] Comparatively, a lesser percentage of respondents chose the eye-for-an-eye dictum as a justification for death penalty (29.9%) (see Fig. 6.19). Both males and females followed this trend and there was little difference in their reasons for supporting death penalty. Across all age groups, most participants supported the proportionate to wrong done as the reason for supporting

[3]Percentages under reasons for support do not add to 100% since this was a multiple response item.

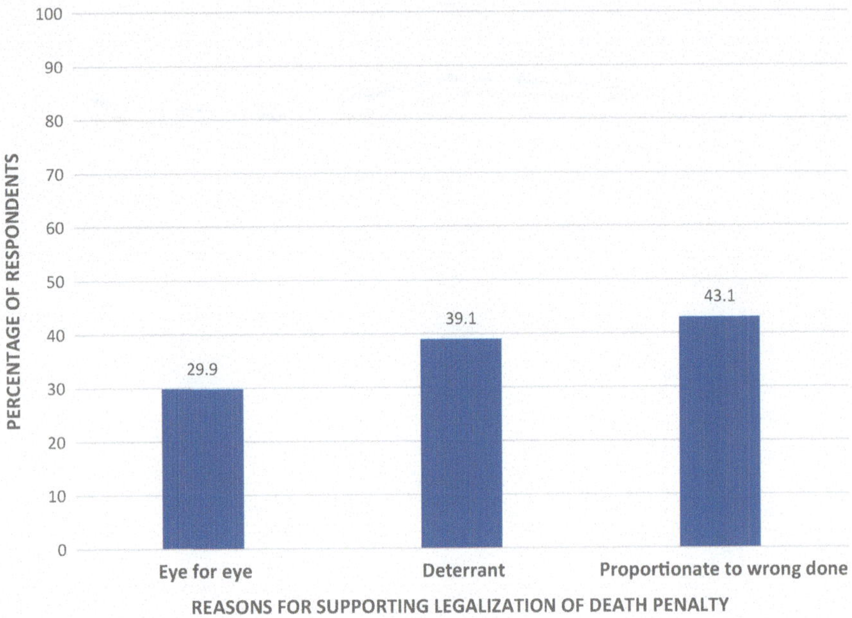

Fig. 6.19 Reasons for favoring legalization of death penalty

death penalty. These findings reflect that overall participants were less supportive of retributive reasons for death penalty.

Support for the deterrence argument increased with increase in educational qualification (from 29.1 to 44.1%), whereas support for the eye-for-an-eye dictum reduced with increase in age (from 31.9 to 21.7%) (see Fig. 6.20) and educational qualification (from 43.9 to 30.9%) (see Fig. 6.21). In addition, those in the older age group showed greater support for the deterrence argument (43.7%). Therefore, with an increase in age and qualification individuals tend to support arguments that appear logical (deterrence) and show decreased support for more impulsive and retributive arguments (eye for an eye). Research in other countries has demonstrated no conclusive evidence for reduction in crime rate due to death penalty. Unlike other countries (especially USA), not much research has been carried out in India to understand the impact of death penalty on crime rate. Thus, the deterrence argument may still be considered as logical by many. For instance, Lambert et al. (2016) found that Indian participants as compared to participants from the USA were more likely to support the deterrence argument for death penalty. It is likely that people in India lack awareness regarding the inability of death penalty to produce a deterrence effect (Lambert et al., 2016), and thus consider it as a reasonable argument to support death penalty. More concrete conclusions can be drawn once studies are exhaustively conducted to understand the impact of death penalty in India.

Among professionals, the lowest support for the "eye-for-an-eye" dictum (19.1%) and the highest support for deterrence (47.9%) were observed. Among Jains (47.1%)

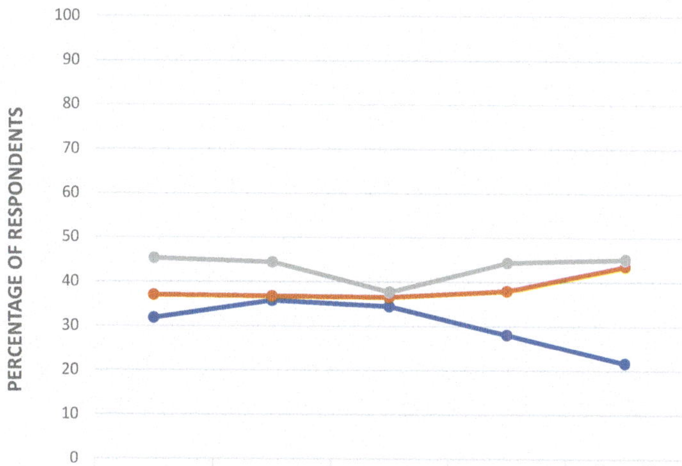

	12-18 years	19-25 years	26-35 years	36 - 45 years	Above 45 years
Eye for eye	31.9	35.8	34.5	28.1	21.7
Deterrant	37.1	36.8	36.6	38	43.7
Proportionate to wrong done	45.3	44.4	37.7	44.3	45.1

Fig. 6.20 Distribution of reasons for favoring legalization of death penalty according to age group

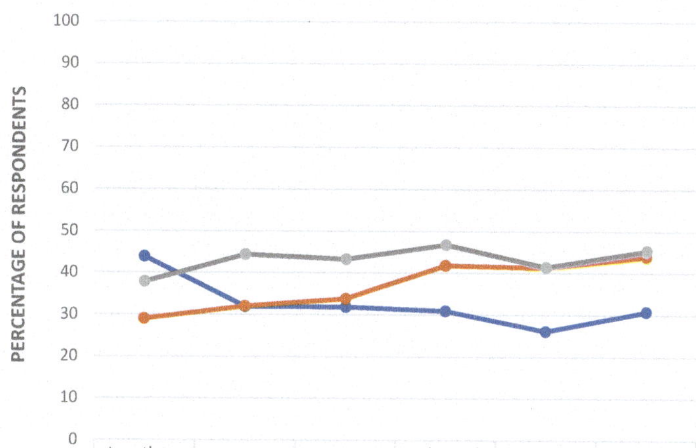

	Less than 10th	10th	12th	Undergraduate	Graduate	Ph.D.
Eye for eye	43.9	32	31.9	31	26.2	30.9
Deterrant	29.1	32.1	33.9	41.9	41.4	44.1
Proportionate to wrong done	37.8	44.3	43.2	46.7	41.4	45.3

Fig. 6.21 Distribution of reasons for favoring legalization of death penalty according to educational qualification

and Buddhists (48.6%), support for the deterrence argument was greater. It is important to note that Buddhist participants were also the ones to show the lowest support for death penalty. Jains (24%) and Christians (26.7%) showed the lowest support for the eye for eye dictum. Responses also suggested that majority of the participants believed that death penalty provides closure to a victim's family (59.9%) and reduces their pain and suffering (64.8%). This is an interesting finding given that only a minority of participants indicated support for retributive arguments (eye for eye dictum) to support death penalty. These responses are also contrary to the contention of several researchers who argued that "closure" is only a theoretical concept which cannot be achieved in the true sense (Adcock, 2010; Madeira, 2010). On the other hand, some researchers proposed that closure is attained by victims' families in other ways such as forgiveness of the perpetrator[4] (Berns, 2009; King, 2003). For instance, an Indian newspaper (Express Web Desk, 2018b) quoted the sister of the victim, Jessica Lal,[5] who was murdered at a socialite party:

> It will be like a catharsis to forgive and move on. I also need to get on with my life...I don't want to hold on to any more anger or hurt. I feel that he has served his sentence. I don't feel there is any need to hanker about the situation.

Therefore, there is no conclusive evidence for achievement of closure after death penalty.

6.4.2.2 Crimes for Which Death Penalty Should Be Legalized

From the list of crimes provided majority of the participants wanted death penalty to be legalized for rape (77. 7%) and murder (64%) (see Fig. 6.22). Irrespective of age, gender, educational qualification, profession, and religion, rape and murder were the crimes for which majority of the participants indicated the need for legalization of death penalty. The demand for death penalty in the case of rape can be understood by considering the recent scenario of crime against women in India. There was considerable media, political, and public attention drawn toward violence against women (specifically rape) after the *Nirbhaya* gang rape case in 2012.[6] Large groups of individuals protested and demanded death penalty for the perpetrators (Indo-Asian News Service, 2017). Given these circumstances, it is possible that this significant rape incident influenced the participants' responses. The findings of this study are also supported by a recent incident related to a rape case of a female minor, namely, the *Kathua* rape case. After much public outrage over this case, the President of India signed an ordinance which approved death penalty for rape of females under the age

[4]For more research on "closure," refer to the chapter on "Psychosocial Factors Associated with Death Penalty" in this book.

[5]For details of the Jessica Lal case see http://indianexpress.com/article/what-is/what-is-the-jessica-lal-murder-case/.

[6]For details of Nirbhaya case https://www.mid-day.com/articles/national-news-nirbhaya-rape-case-verdict-flashback-dark-night-of-december-16-2012-delhi/18226167.

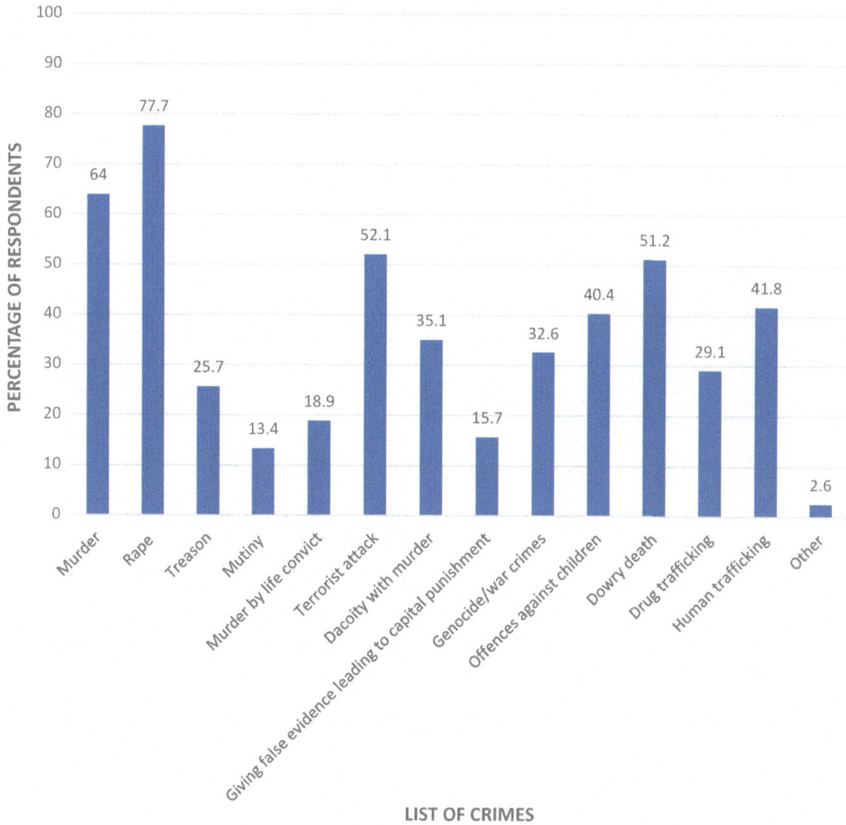

Fig. 6.22 Crimes for which death penalty should be legalized

of 12 years (Express Web Desk, 2018a). This is indicative of the public inclination toward harsher punishments for rape in India.

6.4.3 Opposition Toward Death Penalty

Majority of the participants who were against death penalty indicated that death penalty should be abolished since it violates the right to life (54.1%) and is barbaric and inhumane (47.4%) (see Fig. 6.23). No significant differences in the reasons selected were found across different groups based on age, gender, education, and profession. Buddhists held a slightly different viewpoint as majority indicated that death penalty should be legalized since it violates the right to life (63.8%) and acts against poor and socially vulnerable individuals (44.8%). Participants were divided in their opinion on whether delay in decision-making was a sufficient reason to

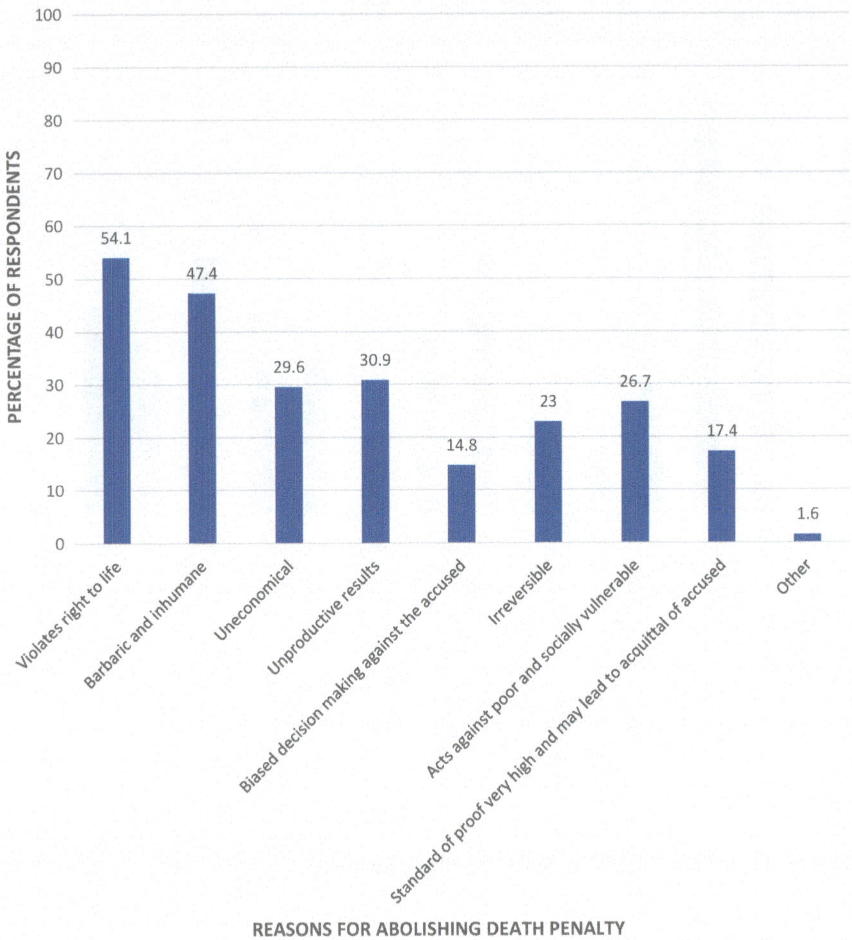

Fig. 6.23 Reasons for not favoring legalization of death penalty

abolish death penalty and whether an abolition would bring the crime rates down. A large percentage of participants also believed that the judicial system is susceptible to errors to an extent that an innocent may be given death penalty (26.6% strongly agreed and 33.4% agreed). Therefore, it can be concluded that participants supported the abolition of death penalty from a human rights and morality perspective.

6.5 Conclusion

The present study was an attempt to provide an overview of public opinion on death penalty based on a large sample from the Indian population (N = 25,210). The findings indicated major support for death penalty. The support for death penalty increased with age and decreased with increase in educational qualification. Some differences based on religion were also observed which can be explored further by future researchers. Buddhist participants distinctly showed less support, whereas Hindu, Muslim, and Sikh participants showed more support for death penalty. It is important to highlight that since support was measured as a dichotomous variable ("yes" or "no" response), the level or degree of support/opposition of death penalty was not clearly captured. Previous studies in India have utilized a Likert-type scale which could be a helpful alternative to understand the strength of the support to death penalty by the public. (Lambert et al., 2008). Furthermore, the highest support for death penalty was seen in the case of rape and murder crimes. This indicates that individuals are in favor of death penalty only for certain crimes and not the others. The impact of death penalty on crime rates in India has not been investigated, yet the public primarily supported death penalty as they believed it is proportionate to the wrong done and has a deterrence effect. Support for deterrence increased with an increase in educational qualification and age and that for the eye-for-an-eye dictum decreased with increase in educational qualifications and age. On the other hand, those who opposed death penalty believed that it violates the right to life of an individual and is inhumane. The results of this study should be interpreted with caution since death penalty attitudes were examined with respect to demographic variables. Research has shown that demographic variables are related to death penalty opinions due to attitudinal variables that underlie them as, for example, religious orientation, racial bias, punitiveness, etc. (Barkan & Cohn, 2005). This research did not explore these attitudinal variables; therefore, the results need to be interpreted in the light of these limitations.

References

Adcock, C. F. (2010). The collateral anti-therapeutic effects of the death penalty. *Florida Coastal Law Review, 11*(2), 289–320.

Alasti, S., & Bronson, E. (2017). Death penalty in Sharia law. In R. M. Bohm & G. Lee (Eds.), *Routledge handbook on capital punishment* (pp. 231–244). New York NY: Routledge.

Applegate, B. K., Cullen, F. T., & Fisher, B. S. (2002). Public views toward crime and correctional policies: Is there a gender gap? *Journal of Criminal Justice, 30*(2), 89–100.

Barkan, S. E., & Cohn, S. F. (2005). On reducing white support for the death penalty: A pessimistic appraisal. *Criminology & Public Policy, 4*(1), 39–44.

Baumer, E. P., Messner, S. F., & Rosenfeld, R. (2003). Explaining spatial variation in support for capital punishment: A multilevel analysis. *American Journal of Sociology, 108*(4), 844–875.

Berns, N. (2009). Contesting the victim card: Closure discourse and emotion in death penalty rhetoric. *The Sociological Quarterly, 50*(3), 383–406.

Bohm, R. M. (1991). American death penalty opinion, 1936–1986: A critical examination of the Gallup polls. In R. M. Bohm (Ed.), *The death penalty in America: Current research* (pp. 113–145). Cincinnati: Anderson Publishing Co.

Burstein, P. (2003). The impact of public opinion on public policy: A review and an agenda. *Political Research Quarterly, 56*(1), 29–40.

Butler, L., Unnever, J. D., Cullen, F. T., & Thielo, A. J. (2017). Public opinion about death penalty. In R. M. Bohm & G. Lee (Eds.), *Routledge handbook on capital punishment* (pp. 55–70). New York NY: Routledge.

Census of India. (2011a). Gender composition. Retrieved from http://censusindia.gov.in/2011-prov-results/data_files/mp/06Gender%20Composition.pdf.

Census of India. (2011b). C-1 population by religious community. Retrieved from http://www.censusindia.gov.in/2011census/C-01.html.

Epstein, L. (2012). On the importance of public opinion. *Daedalus, 141*(4), 5–8.

Express Web Desk. (2018a, April 22). President Ram Nath Kovind approves ordinance awarding death penalty for child rape. *The Indian Express*. Retrieved form http://indianexpress.com/article/india/president-ram-nath-kovind-approves-ordinance-awarding-death-penalty-for-child-rape-5147056/.

Express Web Desk. (2018b, April 24). What is the Jessica Lal murder case? *The Indian Express*. Retrieved form http://indianexpress.com/article/what-is/what-is-the-jessica-lal-murder-case/.

Fox, J. A., Radelet, M. L., & Bonsteel, J. L. (1990). Death penalty opinion in the post-Furman years. *NYU Review of Law & Social Change, 18*(2), 499–528.

Hood, R. (2015, July). *World-wide abolition of capital punishment: A human rights imperative.* Lecture delivered at an event organized by Law Commission of India, New Delhi. Retrieved from http://lawcommissionofindia.nic.in/Speech.pdf.

Indo-Asian News Service. (2017, May 6). Nirbhaya rape case: What happened on that dark fateful night of December 16, 2012. *Mid-day*. Retrieved from https://www.mid-day.com/articles/national-news-nirbhaya-rape-case-verdict-flashback-dark-night-of-december-16-2012-delhi/18226167.

Jha, P. (2013, July 24). Many against death penalty. *The Hindu*. Retrieved from http://www.thehindu.com/news/national/many-against-death-penalty/article4949078.ece.

Kamble, S., & Mullet, E. (2014). Young Indians' views on the appropriateness of the death penalty as a function of circumstances of crime: A preliminary study. *Psicológica, 35*(3), 601–611.

King, R. (2003). *Don't kill in our names: Families of murder victims speak out against the death penalty*. New Jersey, USA: Rutgers University Press.

Lambert, E. G., Baker, D. N., Elechi, O. O., Jiang, S., Khondaker, M. I., Pasupuleti, S., et al. (2016). Gender and cultural differences on death penalty support and views among Indian and US college students. *Journal of Ethnicity in Criminal Justice*, 1–18. https://doi.org/10.1080/15377938.2015.1015195.

Lambert, E. G., Pasupuleti, S., Jiang, S., Jaishankar, K., & Bhimarasetty, J. V. (2008). Views on the death penalty among college students in India. *Punishment & Society, 10*(2), 207–218.

Madeira, J. L. (2010). "Why Rebottle the Genie?": Capitalizing on closure in death penalty proceedings. *Indiana Law Journal, 85*(4), 1477–1525.

Miller, M. K., & Hayward, R. D. (2008). Religious characteristics and the death penalty. *Law and Human Behavior, 32*(2), 113–123.

Sato, M. (2013). Public attitudes towards the death penalty. In M. Sato (Ed.), *The death penalty in Japan: Will the public tolerate abolition?* (pp. 37–62). Berlin: Springer Science & Business Media.

Stack, S. (2000). Support for the death penalty: A gender-specific model. *Sex Roles, 43*(3/4), 163–179.

Stack, S. (2004). Public opinion on the death penalty. *International Criminal Justice Review, 14*(1), 69–98.

Times of India. (2018). *Polls*. Retrieved from https://timesofindia.indiatimes.com/home/polls?curpg=4.

United Nations General Assembly. (2010). Report of the working group on the universal periodic review: Belarus. U.N. Doc. A/HRC/15/16. Retrieved from http://lib.ohchr.org/HRBodies/UPR/Documents/Session8/BY/A.HRC.15.16.Add.1_BELARUS_eng.pdf.

Vidmar, N., & Ellsworth, P. (1974). Public opinion and the death penalty. *Stanford Law Review, 26*(6), 1245–1270.

Vollum, S., Longmire, D. R., & Buffington-Vollum, J. (2004). Confidence in the death penalty and support for its use: Exploring the value-expressive dimension of death penalty attitudes. *Justice Quarterly, 21*(3), 521–546.

Widony, A., & Hammer, R. (2009). *The effects of education and race on attitudes about capital punishment.* Unpublished manuscript, Oregon State University, USA. Retrieved from http://people.oregonstate.edu/~hammerr/soc316/Education_Race_and_Capital_Punishment.pdf.

Winright, T. (2017). Christianity and the death penalty. In R. M. Bohm & G. Lee (Eds.), *Routledge handbook on capital punishment* (pp. 201–217). New York NY: Routledge.

Young, R. L. (1991). Race, conceptions of crime and justice, and support for the death penalty. *Social Psychology Quarterly, 54*(1), 67–75.

Chapter 7
A Way Forward

This chapter represents the summary of the book and the way forward for India. In the modern era, the death penalty is a violation of the right to life. The evidence in a vast and diverse country like India points to a strong support for corporeal punishment. We all know that the classic arguments in favor of death penalty have always been retribution and deterrence. But as early as 1764, Cesare Beccaria noticed weaknesses in these arguments and since then new arguments have surfaced justifying the abolition of the death penalty. His book *On Crimes and Punishments* advocated the replacement of the old regime of punishment. However, according to an Amnesty International report, the idea of abolition seems to be slowly gaining support among Indian legal elites and the general populace. From a global perspective, the movement to abolish the death penalty began in the eighteenth century Europe. It is still embedded in many of the statute books because of religion-based culture and its supposed deterrent effects. Today, there have been a growing number of human rights movements and international treaties manifesting the abolition of death penalty. It was only in 1982 that the Protocol to the European Convention on Human Rights calling for the abolition of death penalty was opened for signature. And it was not until 1977 that the General Assembly of the United Nations called for its abolition. The World Day against the Death Penalty is observed on the 10th of October. The most important treaty provision relating to death penalty at the international level is Article 6 of the International Covenant on Civil and Political Rights (ICCPR).

The focus of the book has been on several realms. It also gives us the opportunity to reflect on the situation at the global as well as the national level. In the first chapter, the author provides a global view of the legal status of corporeal punishment. The author digs deeper into providing the continentwise approach by different member states of different conventions and international law instruments. The author also traces data and statistical reports to analyze and discuss the global view of corporeal punishment. In the end, the author discusses the relationship between religious teachings and death penalty. The second chapter specifically looks into the Indian context of death penalty.

S. P. Sahni and M. Junnarkar, *The Death Penalty*,
https://doi.org/10.1007/978-981-15-3129-3_7

In the first chapter, the author explores the laws and regulations regarding the usage of death penalty. Corporeal punishment of death penalty is mostly given by countries for the most heinous crime committed. The debate on this issue has been going on for a long time. A majority of countries have abolished the death penalty for all the crimes. But certain major countries such as the United States of America, China, Japan, and Singapore do retain death penalty and perform it on the convicts. Some countries have constitution and penal laws that do not provide for death penalty. These are known as de jure abolitionists. And other countries where courts do not impose the statutory death penalty, those are known as abolitionists in practice or de facto abolitionists. There are countries which have abolished the death penalty completely for all crimes such as Fiji in 2015 as well as Republic of Congo, and Madagascar The most recent countries to join this category are Guinea and Mongolia in 2017 (Amnesty International, 2018). A moratorium is a mechanism that the international law provides for strengthening de facto abolition. This guarantees that the state representative on the trial commits not to request the death penalty.

The author starts the chapter with the continentwise approach. In the African continent, 38 states out of the 54 are abolitionist states. There has been a significant reduction in the number of executions carried out in the region. In the recent years, the Sub-Saharan Africa has seen a positive progress on the abolition of the death penalty. The progress is seen significant as Africa was depicted as the most troubled continent just two decades ago. Africa's retention of the death penalty has been linked with the country's colonial oppression and repression. The traditional laws in the country were more imbued with human values than the laws that influenced them. The influences on Africa were Anglo-American, Roman, Dutch, Islamic, and Coptic laws and they all contained provisions for death penalty. It was considered to be an effective means of forcing local people into submission. The North African country of Tunisia has been execution-free since 1991 and is also one of the first countries in the region to adopt this practice. The Supreme Court of South Africa was newly constituted in 1995 which gave a few landmark judgments. The pro-execution government, on the other hand, had executed 164 people in 1987 alone. The death penalty was applied and executed for crimes such as rape, murder, housebreaking, robbery, or attempted robbery with aggravating circumstances, kidnapping, terrorism, and treason. Most political crimes were also punished with the death sentence. However, the decision of the abolishment came from the Supreme Court case of State v Makwanyane and Mchunu, 1985 where the apex court after hearing both sides outlawed death penalty. It was outlawed because it breached the most fundamental human rights and the right to life. The current debate among the lawmakers and the public of South Africa is whether the country needs to incorporate the death penalty back into the system. This is because of the rise in crimes such as aggravated robbery, which has risen from 232 to 354 (by 52%) (South African Institute of Race relations, 2016). In southern Africa, some countries such as Algeria, due to the rise in the number of heinous crimes, included references to the death penalty. Egypt, on the other hand, still remains one of the states to adopt usage of death penalty for crimes such as murder, rape as well as offences related to drug trafficking. The Sub-Saharan Africa has witnessed a rapid increase in the number of death sentences even though the number of death sentences imposed by the Courts has actually dipped from 21 in 2015 to 17 in 2016.

The current death penalty scene in the United States began in the year 1976 when the Supreme Court declared it as not being unconstitutional. This decision was in conjunction with an important ruling a decade later (McCleskey v. Kemp, 1987) which settled the constitutionality of death penalty. In America, out of 35 independent American states, which are members to the United Nations Charter, 37% of these states maintain death penalty in both law and practice, 14% only allow in exceptional cases such as wartime, 3% have not used in the last 10 years, and the rest 46% have completely abolished it (Cornell Center on the Death Penalty Worldwide, N.D). Out of the 50 states, death penalty still exists in the 31 states while the rest 19 states have completely abolished it from their legal system. A majority of the general public has shown support for the death penalty as a legitimate punishment for murder, in some instances. These have steadily increased from around 65% in the early 1970s. Before the case of Furman v Georgia (Polsby, 1972), where the Supreme Court ruled that arbitrary imposition of the death penalty was cruel and unconstitutional, most of the cases of death penalty were considered to be more of a racial bias, as Black defendants were more likely to be sentenced to death than White defendants.

The state of California has also witnessed a long battle on the reinstatement of death penalty after the voters opted for it in 1978. They imposed many death sentences but executed very few. The state of New Hampshire also had the law on the books but imposed no death sentences after 1976. States such as Texas, Oklahoma or Virginia have the law, impose sentences and carry out the execution as well. There are 15 other states where capital punishment does not exist legally. There are a lot of variations within the country with regard to capital punishment law and practice. The California State Senate established the California Commission on the Fair Administration of Justice in 2004, a bipartisan blue-ribbon panel, tasked with speeding up the death penalty process, investigating the causes of wrongful convictions and executions in the state, and recommending reforms. The resulting report made substantive recommendations for change. Since 1976, 83% of all executions have been carried out in only nine states namely Virginia, Texas, Oklahoma, North and South Carolina, Alabama, Florida, and Georgia. The maximum executions have taken place in Texas.

In Canada, capital punishment was removed from the Canadian Criminal Code in 1976. This was replaced by a mandatory life sentence without the possibility of parole for 25 years for all first-degree murders. Before 1976, crimes such as murder, treason, and rape carried death penalty. It was in 1962, that the last execution took place in Canada. It was limited only to the killings of on-duty police officers and prison guards. The bill to remove the capital punishment was passed by a free vote in the House of Commons. However, it still remained in the Canadian National Defence Act for the most serious military offences, including treason and mutiny. In 1998, the Canadian National Defence Act was changed to remove the death penalty and replaced it with life imprisonment (Death Penalty in Canada, Amnesty International).

The author then discusses about the scenario of death penalty in the Asia–Pacific region. The Asia–Pacific region continues to have a disproportionate nature when it comes to retaining and implementing death penalty. There are 13 countries that have retained death penalty for ordinary crimes, 1 is abolitionist for ordinary crimes, 10 are abolitionist in practice, 17 are abolitionist for all crimes, and 28 have abolished the death penalty in law and/or practice. The two Special Administrative Regions of China—Hong Kong and Macau—have separate criminal law and justice systems and are abolitionist for all crimes (Anti-Death Penalty Asia Network, N.D.). Out of the total Asia–Pacific and Middle Eastern countries, China, Iran, Iraq, Saudi Arabia, and Vietnam had the most confirmed executions in 2018 (Amnesty International Global Report: Death Sentences and Executions 2018). In India, the landmark judgment in the case of *Bachan Singh v. State of Punjab*, addressed the notion of constitutionality of death penalty. The concept of "rarest of the rare" cases has been adopted by the Indian Judiciary since then. The cases of extreme brutality, gross murders, or mass killings have been seen to attract more of the pronouncement of death penalty in India.

The Middle East Islamic states such as Saudi Arabia do have strict laws for death penalty. Saudi Arabia is among the top three nations with the most number of executions, only after China and Iran. Iran has also the world's highest number of executions by stoning.

The picture of the European continent is pretty different compared to all other continents. Here, 96% of the states have abolished death penalty and only 4% still allow both in law and practice. The Council of Europe and the European Union have both declared that the death penalty has no legitimate place in the penal systems of the modern civil societies. By the early years of the twentieth century, 11 European countries got rid of death penalty for all crimes committed in peacetime.

Death penalty or capital punishment is regarded as the most contentious punitive practice in today's society. In the past, death penalty involved punishment like beheading, hanging, etc. In countries like USA or Russia, many other ways like gas chambers, injecting chemicals, etc. were used. But in India, in recent times the demand for death penalty has risen for various crimes like rape, smuggling, etc. Various State Governments like Punjab made legislation of death penalty for drug smugglers. Similarly, states like Madhya Pradesh made legislation for death penalty in rape cases of minor girls, gang rapes, etc. Recently, the Supreme Court acquitted four persons who were innocent but were given death penalty or capital punishment. The debate about abolishing death penalty has again reopened in India with the arrest of Ajmal Kasab, the only 26/11 attacker to be caught alive. He was hanged later.

The fourth chapter presents how public opinion influences greatly the discourse on the death penalty. This chapter discusses how India follows the "rarest of rare" doctrine. But there is no statutory definition of "rarest of rare." This decision came into effect with two landmark judgments of Rajendra Prasad v State of UP in 1979 and Bachan Singh v State of Punjab in 1980. During Mahatma Gandhi's assassination trial, his two sons appealed to the government on the day that the guilty should not be hanged as Mahatma Gandhi did not believe in death sentence. The chapter also highlights how the judges are inadequate to represent public opinion. It has been observed that 40% of Indian people favored life imprisonment over death penalty. The chapter also points out how the use of public opinion polls can be an inadequate measure to understand the complexities of the death penalty. With the examples of

Sheena Bora murder case of 2012 and the Arushi Talwar murder case of 2008, the author highlights how media plays a significant role in the criminal justice system of the country.

The chapter on the "Role of Non-State Actors in Death Penalty" illustrates how the non-state actors which are by definition individuals or organizations that are not affiliated with, directly, or funded through the government—have a direct or indirect relevance in the policy-making of the death penalty. In this chapter, the author has explained the role of United Nations Human Rights Office of the High Commissioner, Amnesty International, International Commission Against Death Penalty, World Coalition Against Death Penalty, Sant'Egidio, criminologists, and media. United Nations Human Rights Office of the High Commissioner aims at universal abolition of the death penalty. The General Assembly, through a series of resolutions, has urged the states to respect international standards that protect the rights of the people facing death penalty. There was also a signed appeal by 12 UN Member States focussing on the need to abolish death penalty in the twenty-first century. According to Amnesty International, death penalty violates the right to life and it holds a strong opposition to death penalty irrespective of the nature of crimes. In 2017, Amnesty International nurtured a landmark *Declaration of Stockholm,* which is the first international abolitionist manifesto on the death penalty. Amnesty International has also set up local groups to promote the importance of human rights, educate people on these issues and abolish the death penalty. The International Commission against Death Penalty (ICDP) is an initiative by the Spanish Government. Along with the aim to abolish death penalty, The International Commission against Death Penalty (ICDP) also insists on helping vulnerable groups of society such as juvenile offenders, pregnant women, and mentally ill in their struggles against death penalty. ICDP participates in various meetings and seminars to further the discourse on death penalty. It has also launched publication "How States abolish the Death Penalty: 29 Case-Studies" wherein there was detailed journey of the 26 countries and the 3 USA states toward their destination of abolishing death penalty. World Coalition Against Death Penalty (WCADP) came into existence in 2002 with the aim to bring all the abolitionist organizations under one umbrella by encouraging cooperation and formulation of common strategies. Along with keeping track of data and figures, WCADP also mobilizes people, from an individual to mass level, by organizing outreach and awareness programs. The community of Sant'Egidio is a religious organization that mainly focusses on death rows and the fight against capital punishment. The purpose of the organization is to reach out to death row prisoners and offer them support and assistance in their journey. The author then presents the view of famous Italian criminologist from the classical school, Cesare Beccaria, who was against death penalty. He regarded the practice of death penalty as against the humanitarian principle. It did not serve the purpose in deterring crime in society. His views were largely opposed by another Italian Criminologist, Cesare Lombrosso, who was inspired by Darwin's evolution theory. Lombroso's main argument was that criminals are evolutionary throwbacks who were inferior to non-criminals and this is what he called the idea of atavism. In this chapter, the author has highlighted the various researches that have found that death penalty has no deterrence value. Criminologists around the world agree on this view to help facilitate the legal policies and provide the basis for court rulings. Lastly, the author introduces the role of media in shaping the views of the common men regarding death penalty. Facts and figures show that there is a close match between pro-abolitionist and pro-retentionist in this century. The author also highlighted the various sections of media wherein one section presents the pros and cons of death penalty while the other section is focussed on generating Television Rating Points (TRP's), by providing sensational cases that sway away from the real nuanced version of the story and get tangled with variations to please the normative views and opinions. The author concludes the chapter by pointing at the relevance of death penalty and the salient role these non-state actors play in influencing the perspective on death penalty around the world.

In the chapter "Psychosocial factors associated with Death Penalty: *Impact on Families of Victims, Families of Defendants and the 'Others'*," the author presents review of literature about the several perceptions and psychosocial impact of death sentence on the families of victims, families of the defendants and other groups who interact with a capital defendant. The author in the first section provides various researches where it was found that families of death penalty victims experience guilt and indulge in self-blame for not being able to protect the victim. There is also evidence of feeling disappointment coupled with frustrations and distress toward the criminal justice system. The author then further presents three models to explain the experiences of victims' families. The first model is the explanation of how PTSD occurs and maintains in victims' families with the help of Mowler's Two Factor Learning Theory. Through this theory, it was explained how the repeated exposure to the presentation of trauma and criminal justice system can increase their risk to the development of PTSD-like symptoms. The author then explains how the normal grieving process gets complicated when it is associated with constant media scrutiny. Their mournin gets witnessed by public eyes which further puts at risk their grieving process. The author also discusses the concept of closure in victims' families. Closure can vary from family to family—some families experience closure by forgiveness while others experience closure by punishing the perpetrators. The author points out the discrimination faced by various victim family groups such as "Murder Victims," "Families for Reconciliation," and movements such as "Declaration to Life" on the ground that they actively advocate the abolishment of death penalty. The defendants' families experience distress on several levels ranging from facing biased and unjust treatment from the criminal justice system to being shunned by the society. The role of media in providing lurid details of the perpetrator keeps the defendants' families' stories unknown to the masses. The inimical effect of the death penalty on children of death row prisoners is a matter in question presented by the author. These children are at higher risks of substance abuse, truancy, violence, and mental health issues. The author compares the experiences of victim's and offender's families by drawing special attention to the similar struggles both families' go through ranging from facing trauma and grief to facing financial and legal expenses. The author has also drawn attention to how the defendant families' grief is distinct from the victim families'. Their grief is anticipatory in nature and their concerns are usually negated by the society. They also receive limited assistance and support from the government.

There is a need to pay heed to the limited amount of research being done on the experience of "others" in death penalty cases. These "others" refer to the wardens, guards of the prison, death row lawyers, jurors, and mental health practitioners. The author details the experiences of jurors and lawyers who face frustrations due to the responsibility to make the decision as well as exposure to graphic details of the crime. The jurors have been found to experience "Post-jury blues" which refer to the nightmares, sleep disturbances, and loss of appetite following a capital trial. Even lawyers of the death penalty cases face ongoing trauma and ongoing cycle of despair and stress. Similar reactions are experienced by prison staff, executioner, and the prisoner on death row. They are more prone to PTSD symptoms due to the high level of psychological and physical impact of witnessing executions. Lastly, the author presents the experiences of execution witnesses which include the executioners, medical specialists, journalists, volunteers and in some cases, families of victims, and the death row prisoners. The author concludes by highlighting the trauma and distress faced by these people through various researches that have been conducted and also draws special attention to the public witnessing of executions.

In the chapter "Public *Opinion on Death Penalty: An Indian Study,*" the author presents a study that was conducted by Jindal Institute of Behavioural Sciences in India to understand the opinion of public on death penalty. The study was conducted keeping in mind the gaps in previous researches in India that failed to capture the generalizability of their studies. The sample of the study consisted of 25,210 participants of which 14,100 were males and 9,515 females in the age range of 12–80 years. Majority of the people had post-graduation as their highest educational qualification. The study was employed by a self-administered survey questionnaire that comprised of 17 questions. The questionnaire was divided into three parts. The first section covered the demographic information and the basic opinion of the participants on the death penalty in India. Part A of the questionnaire dealt with the reasons for supporting death penalty and the kind of crimes for which death penalty should be legalized. Part B of the questionnaire explored the reasons for supporting abolishment of death penalty. Descriptive analysis of the study found that 80% of the participants indicated support for death penalty and 20% were not in favor of its legalization. The results were further analyzed with respect to all the demographic variables. The study found out that there was a decrease in support toward the death penalty legalization, with the advancement in educational qualifications. Analysis of the public opinion based on religious affiliation showed that Hindus (81.8%) were the greatest supporters of death penalty. On the other hand, Buddhist respondents (65.5%) were the least supportive of death penalty.

The second part focuses on the present Indian context with respect to the death penalty. The author discusses the various significant changes that have taken place with respect to the policy change and the legal debate around the topic. In the years between 1998 and 2007, India has executed only one person (in 2004). India's death penalty has been shaped by various social, political, and economic factors. India is divided by caste and religion. India has had a long history of using death as a capital punishment. The age-old tradition of caste was one of the major deciding factors to prescribe punishment. India has a long history of capital punishment under the Mughal dynasty as well as the British rule. A Sudra (a person belonging to a depressed caste) who insulted a Brahmin (priest) faced death whereas a Brahmin who killed a Sudra would get away with just a fine. The death penalty in India still remains a caste and class-inflicted punishment (Muralidhar, 1998; Clifford, 2004; Batra, 2007).

There have been significant challenges since 2017. There has also been emergence of the constitutional regulation of death penalty in India with the "rarest of the rare" doctrine being decided by the Court. India followed the "worst of the worst" framework from the Furman v. Georgia case. This chapter also presents an overview on the pre-constitutional history of death penalty, the current position, and the ongoing changes till date. The Law Commission of India has attempted to analyze the need for death penalty on two separate occasions. The 35th Report called for its retention and described how capital punishment should be the discretion of the Hon'ble Court. In the more recent 262nd report released in August 2015, the Law Commission of India recommended abolition of death penalty except in terror cases. The center as well as state governments have to accept or reject the recommendations. India's execution rate has also been very low when compared to any other retentionist nation in the world. The Constitution of 1950 did not abolish death penalty until the new Code of Criminal Procedure took effect in 1973. The revised code turned death into an exceptional punishment which requires the judges to make the issue of a capital sentence, a separate sentencing phase of the trial. Today, capital cases begun in trial courts at the state level unfold in two stages, first the guilt is determined and then the sentence is decided (Batra, 2008: 50). Section 354(5) of the Code of Criminal Procedure 1973 lays down that all death sentences must be carried out by hanging.

India also has a high threshold for death sentences. There seems to be an absence of cruel and unusual punishment clause and vagueness as well. There are contemporary challenges to the abolition of death penalty and criminal sentencing.

One reason for abolishing death penalty has been with regard to the brutality of its nature. In earlier times, executions involved public spectators and it was not limited to serious crimes. Advocates in support of death penalty view it as necessary to safeguard and protect other citizens. Another reason for the scrapping of death penalty is the debate about capital punishment and human dignity. In understanding the value and dignity of an individual, the power to decide has always rested on the Government.

Dating back to the earliest civilizations of the world like Mesopotamia and Indus Valley civilization, we have seen that the informal judicial system had established many stern laws to punish the guilty. This provided a clear message to all that anyone interfering with the rights of the people would be dealt with seriously. Another alternative to capital punishment is that of life imprisonment which is 14 years as of now in India. Serving out capital punishment also helps in spreading fear in the minds of the people. They will hesitate and restrain from committing crime and being a risk to the lives of other people. Having a country that serves out capital punishment definitely brings about faith in the judicial system of a nation.

When India was formed and Law was introduced in the land, punishments were awarded on the premise to kill the criminal in the person and not the person. We seem to have forgotten what the motto of the judiciary system of India says: "Wherever Dharma prevails, there comes Victory," which roughly translates to restoring order to the society and not eradicating the very person. One must deal with the crime and eradicate it from the criminal. Today, technology is leaping out of bounds and chains, hence why should our judicial system be still plagued with age-old practices. Every individual alive has the right to live and only the giver has the right to take it away, hence no mere immortal shall possess such godly power. We should and will evolve with time and our practices should change with time.

References

Amnesty International (2015). *The death penalty in Saudi Arabia: facts and figures*. Retrieved from https://www.amnesty.org/en/latest/news/2015/08/the-death-penalty-in-saudi-arabia-facts-and-figures/ dated 12th May 2017.

Amnesty International (2018). The Death Penalty in 2017: Facts and Figures. Retrieved from https://www.amnesty.org/en/latest/news/2018/04/death-penalty-facts-and-figures-2017/ dated 4th October 2019.

Amnesty International (2019). Death Penalty in Canada. Retrieved from https://www.amnesty.ca/our-work/issues/death-penalty-support-abolition/death-penalty-canada dated 8th October 2019.

Anti-Death Penalty Asia Network, Fact and figures, N.D. Retrieved from https://adpan.org/ dated 5th October 2019.

Batra, B. J. (2007). The death penalty in India: Issues and aspects. In background paper for the launch seminar on the Sino-EU project. Moving the debate forward on the death penalty in China (pp. 1–28).

Batra, B. (2008). Lethal lottery: the death penalty in India: a study of supreme court judgments in death penalty cases 1950–2006. Tamil Nadu and Puducherry: Amnesty International India and People's Union for Civil Liberties.

Bachan Singh v. State of Punjab, (1980) 2 SCC 684 : 1980 SCC (Cri) 580 para 136.

Clifford, T. (2004). The death penalty in India: a comparative view. Unpublished paper. University of California at Berkeley Boalt Hall School of Law.

Death Penalty Databse, Cornell Center on Death Penalty Worldwide. Retreieved from http://www.worldcoalition.org/Global-overview-of-women-facing-the-death-penalty.html dated 10th October 2019.

Deshwal, S. (2019). Death Penalty: Contemporary Issues. Retrieved from https://www.indianbarassociation.org/death-penalty-contemporary-issues/ dated 4th October 2019.

Muralidhar, S. (1998). "Hang Them Now, Hang Them Not: India's Travails with the Death Penalty". Journal of the Indian Law Institute. Retrieved from www.ielrc.org/content/ a9803.pdf dated 5th May 2019.

Polsby, D. D. (1972). The Death of Capital Punishment? Furman v. Georgia. *The Supreme Court Review*, *1972*, 1–40.

South African Institute of Race Relations (2016). *Capital punishment in South Africa: was abolition the right decision?* Retrieved from https://irr.org.za/reports/occasional-reports/files/draft-2-irr-capital-punishment-in-sa-211116.pdf dated 5th May 2018.

State v Makwanyane and Mchunu, 1985, CCT3/94.